The Trading Psychology Collection

Control Your Inner Trader
Overcome Your Fear in Trading
How to Stop Over-trading

by LR Thomas

Trading the financial markets has large potential rewards but also large potential risks. You must be aware of the risks and be willing to accept them in order to invest in the financial markets. Don't trade with money you can't afford to lose. No representation is made that any account is likely to or will achieve profits or losses similar to any information found in this book. The past performance of any trading system or methodology does not necessarily indicate future results.

Table of Contents

Author Contact Details

Please contact me with any questions or problems you may have about my books. You may contact me via email at lrthomasauthor@gmail.com

List of Books by LR Thomas

Control Your Inner Trader

Overcome Your Fear in Trading

How to Stop Over-trading

The 10XROI Trading System

The Trade Around Your Job System

The High ROI Scalping System

The High ROI End of Day System

Pyramid Your Trades to Profits

Learn to Trade Forex Without Losing Your Shirt

The Challenge of Trading

Most books about trading psychology are very complex: this book is not one of them. Most books about trading psychology describe the difficulties faced by traders but fall short of describing processes to deal with those problems; again this book is not one of those type of books.

This book outlines the challenges traders face with their psychology and then outlines simple strategies to deal with each of those challenges.

The reason I can cover these in a book when I don't know you personally is that the challenges of trading tend to evoke the same behaviors. Let me list those behaviours now so you can see what I mean.

Problem Behaviours in Trading

Entering a trade when there is no trade to take.
Frequently missing trades that you should have taken.
Entering trades too late.
Entering trades too early.
Revenge trading, where you lose control and start trying to make back losses.
Risking too much on a trade.
Risking too little on a trade.
Trading outside their strategy.
Trading without a stop loss.
Moving a stop loss further away
Trading with too tight a stop loss.
Taking profits too early.
Taking profits too late.
Trading too many strategies and mixing them up.
Trading too many time frames and mixing them up

Trading too many pairs.
Being too influenced by other traders
Buying trading course after trading course
Searching for the Holy Grail trading system
Frozen Trigger finger (fear of entering trades)

All the above issues are symptoms of a wrong trading mind set, so why does that happen and what can we do about it.

Let me start with the foundational attitude needed to become a 'Pro' trader. Notice I said 'Pro' trader, I didn't say winning trader. There is a profound difference in attitude between a trader working at increasing professionalism and a trader who wants to be a 'winning' trader. So why should you work at being a pro trader?

Turning Pro

In his book 'The War of Art' a book which I highly recommend you buy, Stephen Pressfield describes the difference between an amateur and a professional. Firstly a professional is not defined by the result of their behaviour but by their seriousness about the process. They have to overcome their inner resistance which is their worst enemy.

'Turning Pro' as defined in his excellent book is a decision to commit no matter what the result. To accept that things will be hard and miserable and boring but your job is to turn up and do your 'work' to the best of your ability.

Pressfield defines 'work' as any activity that improves your life over the long term but in the short term is uncomfortable. However I think his analogy is more applicable to a creative act which is his writing but could easily describe the act of trading. Throughout this book I will describe the desired trading mentality as 'turning pro'.

Trading is the ultimate creative act, our trading systems whether they are our own design or not, require us to make a judgement that we know is ultimately subjective. We decide to risk money on our ideas and we have to decide on when to get in and out of the markets. This requires an independent mind set and a commitment to excellence that most people never make. In other words you have to treat your creative act like a profession. But unlike most professions, you make the rules. You turn pro when you abide by the rules you have made, even when you don't yet know if they are valid.

The problem is that many people get into trading as a way of obtaining freedom from a job or profession. They don't want more professionalism, they want less. They don't want to make rules and stick to them, they want creative freedom. They don't want boring and miserable, they want exciting and happy. These attitudes form their foundational mind set when they get into trading. Is it any wonder that they trade impulsively when their foundation is all messed up.

They look to trading to provide what they are not getting from their lives, they ask of trading what trading is not able to give. They want trading to fill the hole in their lives and to be profitable. Trading cannot do that. Trading is just trading!

If you look to trading to get excitement then trading can give you excitement, but don't expect to be profitable if what you are really looking for is excitement.

If you are looking to trading to fill your time then trading can take up every hour of your time, but don't expect to be profitable if what you are really looking for is a way to fill your time.

If you are looking for a new challenge in life then trading can challenge you as you have never been challenged before, but it doesn't mean you will be profitable.

Do you see where I am going with this, if you got into trading for the wrong reasons, then now is the time to admit it to yourself and consider whether you really want to get further involved in trading. Why should you consider this? Because a professional trader is not looking for excitement or challenge or a way to spend their time, they are simply looking for opportunities to profit in the market.

That is their job and they have to have the exquisite patience to wait for the right opportunity, to wait for the right entry, to wait for the trade to play out, to wait to get to break even and to wait to take profits.

Waiting... waiting is not exciting, it is the most boring thing you can do and it also encourages anxiety among traders who are not pro. This anxiety is what causes behaviours such as taking trades that aren't there or entering a trade too early. Are you prepared to wait, because in trading that is how you will spend the vast majority of your time?

Compare trading to travelling on a bus, firstly when you wait for a bus you know you will have to wait, you accept it. If another bus comes along without your number on the front you let it go by, you don't think 'I don't know if another bus will come along so I better take this bus'. When you do get on the right bus, how do you then spend your time? You don't keep looking out the window to check if the bus is moving, you while away your time reading or doing work or chatting while you wait for the bus to finish its journey. You fully accept the bus journey may be long, you may try and alleviate the boredom by doing some other things while the bus is doing its' thing but you don't try to micro manage the bus journey.

If this analogy doesn't 'speak' to you, then what about fishing? When you see fishermen waiting for the right bite to come and sitting on the bank does that look exciting, yet that is the type of activity that trading really involves.

(Here I will digress for a little and say that this was my biggest problem, I just couldn't wait! I have attention deficit disorder and I have always had problems of impulse control but I wouldn't accept it. I just tried harder but if anything that made the problem worse.

The problem was easily solved by only trading the larger time frames. No more long hours spent staring at the screen! I am not by nature a fisherman.)

Another reason that a lot of people get into trading is that they think it is a route to fast riches, or 'get rich quick'. They may have little money from their job or they need to replace their income and because they have this belief about trading they do things in their trading that a professional trader wouldn't do.

They bet too much on their trades, they are careless about their entries; they let their profits run too far and get whipsawed by the price, losing the profits they have made. They get caught up in revenge trading and eventually get margined out.

Can you see how the wrong beliefs about trading can cause certain types of behaviours? The truth about trading is that most of the rich traders you hear about get rich by trading money for other people.

The richest traders are hedge fund managers and people who own trading houses, highly paid bank traders and other high paid traders at the top of their profession. They earn the big money by getting a performance percentage.

If you want to make big money from the markets, the best route is to become a profitable and professional trader with a proven track record and then go work for a fund or set up your own fund. Here is a link to a Youtube video of a woman who learned to trade options and built a fund of over $140,000,000.

http://tinyurl.com/140million

Can you see the different behaviours it would evoke if your goal was to become a profitable trader and build a track record so you could attract investment, rather than use trading itself as a vehicle for making fast money?

Retail traders working from home, on the whole can make a very good living from the markets if they are successful, however few of them are mega rich.

When you read about these work at home traders you will also see they usually took quite a few years to build up to that level.

The advantage that a retail trader has over the hedge fund manager or bank trader is that they have no accountability to investors or bosses.

This brings me to my next point. Another reason people want to become traders is to have freedom and independence. They are sick of having a boss, or they may have been fired from their job and they want to call the shots in their own life.

Now up to a point trading can provide freedom and independence. You are location independent, anywhere you can get an internet connection is suitable for trading. You have no boss, no employees, no stock, no suppliers and no office politics, none of the usual hassles of working for a boss or running your own business.

The trouble comes when the beliefs about the type of freedom provided by the markets spill over into a trading system. This leads to behaviours like ignoring the rules of your system, missing trades because you fail to check the charts at the appropriate times, chopping and changing between systems, adding one part of a system to another system. After all if the market gives you complete freedom to do what you want then what difference does it make, right?

The truth is that trading can become a harsh task master depending on what trading system you choose, the way to get more freedom is to choose a system with a great amount of freedom built in, such as an end of day or four hour system. (My trading systems Trade around Your Job and The 10XROI Trading System are designed for this).

Many traders make the mistake of choosing a system that requires the same time attendance as a full-time job, or worse. If you are based in the US and you want to trade the London Open, then you have to get up in the early hours of the morning. This is fine if you accept this, but if there is an internal conflict because you are looking for greater freedom in your life then you will indulge in self sabotaging behaviours that can ruin your trading.

The other reason these types of intense day trading systems are difficult to adhere to is due to the amount of time you can maintain emotional self-control. (I go into this in more depth later in the book).

Therefore the areas of trading where you have freedom are in the type of trading system you choose, the instruments you trade and the location you choose.

The areas of trading where you have no freedom are to do with sticking to the rules of the trading system you have chosen, sticking to the money management plan you have chosen, keeping detailed records (in order to practice Kaizen (continuous compounding improvement)

So the first stage to turning pro is to fully accept the true nature of trading, what it is and what it isn't...

If you can accept this you have reached the first stage of becoming a professional trader.

The second stage is to decide whether you truly want to commit to becoming a professional trader. (Remember that doesn't mean a winning trader that means professional in your attitude)

Why is it important to differentiate between being a winning trader and being a professional trader?

The reason is that one is completely within our control and one is completely outside our control. The true professional has faith that if she does her part then the numbers will play out and she will by default become profitable but she has no control over whether the next trade will be a winner or a loser. Therefore to have as a goal to be winning trader or even a profitable trader is inappropriate, that should be built into the trading system you are using.

The goal is to be a professional trader and execute your system as it was meant to be executed when you designed it. That is the only thing you can control and is the only thing that will ensure that your trading becomes profitable over the long term.

Therefore most of your time and focus should be spent on the execution of your system, combined with recording the results. The mind-set is one of Kaizen which is Japanese for "improvement" or "change for the best" and refers to philosophy or practices that focus upon continuous improvement of processes.

Each change in itself may be small, but the compounded effect of many small improvements leads to huge improvements overall. For example, let's say you have a win loss ratio of 40%, that is you win 4 out of ten trades. You discover through keeping rigorous records that you have more winners when you short than when you take longs. You decide to only take shorts and increase your win loss ratio to 55%.

You also find that your normal take profit is 1-2, you intend to stay in the trade longer to take bigger profits but you always get impatient and scared of losing your winnings and exit early in the trade.

Through back testing you find that most of your winning trades would have easily given you a 1-4 reward if you had only stayed in the trade. You put in place techniques (which I will give you later) to stop yourself trying to micro-manage the trade and put in fixed exits of 1-4 Risk Reward Ratio.

What has now happened to your profits, well you turned an unprofitable trading system which only had a 40% win rate and a 1-2 Risk reward to a very profitable system with a 55% win rate and a 1-4 Risk-to-Reward, just by making 2 changes! This is the work of the professional trader, constant improvement of their performance.

Before you go any further in this book, I advise you to take some time to really digest what I have said. Do you really want to commit yourself to turning pro?

It may not be what you really want and there is no shame in that. I listened to an interview once by a trader who had over a 10 year period lost over a million pounds in trading. He'd had a successful business but got the trading bug and because he had the money he just kept blowing out his accounts.

He was still trading 10 years later but I wonder if looking back he would really have chosen that journey.

It seems obvious to me that he wanted challenge in his life and he used trading as a vehicle to get it.

This is what you do not want to happen in your trading career!

Talent Versus Hard Work

So have you decided you want to be a professional trader? Yes?

Then let me ask you another harder question, are you naturally talented at trading?

The prevailing overview is that trading is a learned skill and you don't need talent. That anyone can learn to become anything if they try hard enough. I disagree with this view. I am naturally talented in English, I always got A in my exams without any study, I was also very talented in telephone sales in my younger days, I am not naturally talented in trading.

Some people are naturally talented creatives, some are great singers. When you see real talent you recognise it easily, even in its raw state. That's the job of a talent scout.

If that's the case then why shouldn't this apply to trading as well? Talent makes acquiring a skill a whole lot easier. How can you recognise talent in trading,?

By the amount of time it takes acquire the skills and mind-set needed to perform!

Talented traders need a lot less time. If you hear about a trader who became profitable in less than 2 years then you can be sure that trader has talent.

Now you can become a profitable trader without talent but it will be a longer harder journey.

The woman in this video took 10 years to get to the stage of having a fund of over $140,000,00

http://tinyurl.com/140million

14

The 10,000 Hour Rule

This brings me on to my next point, the 10,000 hour rule. In his excellent book Outliers Malcolm Gladwell talks about the 10,000 hour rule. He cites a study that looked at what top professional musicians did differently from musicians who just went on to become music teachers.

This study found that talent was not a factor, what made the difference was the amount and type of practice. The pro musicians practiced much, much more than the less successful musicians.

Additionally they practiced those areas which would stretch them and make them grow as musicians, the difficult boring stuff, whereas the less committed musicians practiced what felt more comfortable.

So what is the conclusion to this, my view is that some traders have a natural talent that helps shorten the time taken to becoming profitable, however evidence shows that most people who reach the top of their profession do so through having the equivalent of 10,000 hours of the right sort of challenging and stretching practice.

Either way this shows that if you are dedicated you can become successful at trading.

Are you committed? Ok then let's begin.

Creating Your Psychological Foundation

For many traders who have been trading in an out of control fashion for a period of time, they may need to start over and so I am going to start this with that in mind. If you have been trading like this my first advice to you is STOP TRADING NOW!

You need to clear your head and start with a clean slate. By stopping trading for a few weeks and then committing to this process, you can reboot your brain and start over.

Your Trading System

If you have problems because you have too many systems on the go, if you keep skipping from system to system and buying new courses it's time to stop.

The reason traders do this is because of a fear of missing out on the latest greatest system being peddled.

They underestimate the intense focus it takes just to make one strategy profitable. They also equate more systems with more opportunities and more opportunities with making more money.

The problem is that your human brain is limited in the number of things it can focus on at one time. When you try to trade too many time frames, currency pairs or systems you lose clarity, and when you lose clarity you can't trade successfully.

The other issue is that traders try to trade systems and time frames that don't suit their personality and lifestyle. They think because another trader is profitable trading that system then they will be too. However nothing could be further from the truth, you must trade a system that suits you and discard anything that doesn't.

I made this mistake a while back; I bought a course created by a fantastic short term trader with a 94% documented win rate. However I can't trade like her, I have not the patience to stare at the screen during the day. Her method was so different from my own swing trading method that I didn't even bother to follow through with testing the system. I just resolved to stick to what I was good at and not make that mistake again.

How do you know which type of system is right for you? It is the system you seem to have the most success with, that is the easiest and feels most natural.

For me it is the daily and four hour charts and using the hourly charts to fine tune entries. (If you are interested in my methods, try my book the 10XROI trading System or my other books Trade around Your Job and my trade management system that can turn a 1-10 ROI Trade up to a 1-30 ROI trade, Pyramid Your Trades to Profit. They can be found on my author page or see the resource section at the end of this book).

So your first task is to find just one system that suits you and has made you profits in the past. If you have no systems or you are just a beginner then I have some suggestions. Check out my resource page at the end of this book.

When you have one system that works for you, focus on that system and nothing else until you are consistently trading that system to as near perfection as you can.

What is vital is to measure everything so you see where your most profitable trades are and where you lose money. For example you may find that you win many more shorts then longs, so then stop trading longs with the system. Immediately you have improved your profitability.

What type of things can you test, trading shorts only, trading longs only, entry type, entry time of day, days of the week, size of stop and size of take profit, type of entry, and type of exit and much more.

You need to be constantly testing to find the most profitable way to execute your method. So you see why it is more important to find a method that suits you than a fantastically profitable method. You can always tweak to produce a higher return but you can't turn a natural swing trader into a great scalper!

There is no real need to add more systems unless you have very few opportunities in your current one, as if you have a winning system you can make enough money to cover all your wants and needs.

If you do add another system then look for something that easily slots in to your current system so your brain has to do as little adaptation as possible. What do I mean by that? Well in my book the 10XROI System I use the daily charts to find specific entry setups and use the one hour charts to confirm and enter the trade.

In my book 'Trade around Your Job', I am still using daily charts and I am using the same set of circumstances on the daily chart but the entries are different and I use the close of the four hour charts instead of the hourly to enter.

There is enough commonality between the two systems to make it very easy and natural to add on one after having mastered the other.

There is no point trying to master your psychology until you have settled on a proven trading system that suits your lifestyle and personality. When you have found it, then the work begins!

Create the Correct Trading Environment

Firstly I want to explain what I mean by the correct trading environment. It does not just refer to your physical trading space although it certainly includes it.

It relates to everything physical including your actions taken while trading your system. Let me give you an example so you can see what I mean.

Let me relate this to the Trade around Your Job system which uses four hour and daily charts.

Firstly I am lucky enough to have a separate office where my trading platform is situated but you don't need it!

Trading Structure for the Trade around Your Job System

I go into my office and open my charts at 10 pm on Sunday, Monday, Tuesday, Wednesday and Thursday night to look for a daily setup.

I use a specific set of rules to find the correct daily set up. Those rules are in a printed sheet on my wall and on a document on the desk top of my computer.

When I find a daily setup I switch to four hour checking, I check the charts at 8am, 12pm, 4pm, 8pm and 12 am GMT.

If an entry appears, I look at the printed conditions for entry, on my wall or on the desk top to check. If it is a valid entry, I take my calculator and work out how much of my account to risk on this trade.

I then open my trading platform which is different from my charting platform and enter the trade, putting in my stop loss, I also put in a take profit of 7-10 times my risk in case something happens which drives price an unusual amount.

I then set a trading text message alert for 5 times my risk, I then close the platform, close the trading computer and do something else. (I force myself to do this even though I really want to stay and stare at the charts. I know if I do that I am likely to get anxious and exit the trade by talking myself out of it.)

If the text alert goes off I reopen the platform and start trailing my stop loss depending on the different factors which I outline in my Trade around Your Job book.

At 10pm I open the charts again to check for a daily setup and check the progress of my trade.

If the correct price action has taken place I will move my stop loss to break even.

The following day I will check the charts at 10pm where I also look for more daily setups and if applicable I trail the stop loss I will repeat this checking until I am stopped out. I then bring up my trading records and create a physical record of the trade in my trading record book and an excel spread sheet.

I have created a physical structure comprising a set of behaviours in a physical place (my office) based around The Trade Around Your Job System.

The 'Trade Around Your Job' system trades take place around 2-6 times per month. I have structured my set of behaviours to spend as little time as possible at the computer screen. These behaviours form a physical structure that I focus on.

If I find a flaw in this structure, or if I am not able to adhere to this structure, then I work on tweaking the structure or my behaviours so I can act in as robotic and structured a manner as possible. This structure provides the physical success environment for my trading. My focus and aim is to create an environment and set of behaviours that allow me to stick as closely as possible to my trading plan. I also have other structures related to other parts of my trading.

So what does this mean to you? Well in step one, you made sure you had a trading system that fitted your trading style.

In step two, you create a physical environment that allows you to trade this system as perfectly as is humanly possible. One of the purposes of your trading records is to find the stumbling blocks in your behaviour and in your system that prevent you from doing this.

Remove Your Focus

It is also wise to have other absorbing activities that take you away from the charts so your mind is automatically switched to something else. I know of two husband and wife traders who work in IT and both work at their computers full time. When a trade setup comes via software that they created, they take the trade and just continue with their job. What is fantastic about this is that the professional detachment is built in both by removing their focus and by not having to financially depend on trading.

I know another day-trader who plays computer games while waiting for a setup, all the excitement and adrenaline that losing day traders search for, is provided by the game so the actual taking of the trade can be done as professionally as possible.

Overcoming your Faulty Trading Behaviours

You should find at this stage that you are already beginning to think about trading in a more professional fashion. You should have a more realistic view of what trading can and can't give you and you should have set your trading goal.

Your first trading goal should be to create a consistent set of behaviours and to tweak your system until it is profitable.

Notice that this goal is a process goal and not a results goal; you have full control over process goals.

You need to completely forgo results thinking and instead adopt process thinking. If you focus on being the very best trader you can and have faith that if you do this you will become profitable by default then you are thinking right.

Remember, this process involves Kaizen, continuous small improvements compounded to make huge positive changes. Even if when you start, your system is at break even or even losing a little bit, by using these methods you know that you can turn the system into a winning formula.

It is vital that you keep records about everything you can when taking a trade because the better the information you have the more targeted the changes you can make.

It is also very important to start being aware of your thoughts when you are around your trading platform. If you are at the beginning of this process, either because you are a beginning trader or a trader that has had to take a break because you have gone so far off track, then my suggestion is that you go back to demo trading or use a micro – account.

This will save you money and make sure that you are profitable before you add money to your account. If after reading this you feel inner resistance because you want to make money fast, then you are not thinking like a pro trader.

You want to root out those thoughts and bring them to light. They will tell you what stage you are at in the journey from amateur to pro.

The 'trading pro' is self –aware and you need to be aware of your thoughts in order to change them.

You need to be able to mentally stand aside from yourself in order to observe your thoughts rather than just think them. How do you take control of your mind in this way? Daily meditation!

There are different types of meditation; however the one you want to do is the simple clearing of your mind type. Simply sit comfortably for a period of time, say you start with 5 minutes, and then build it up to about 30 minutes a day. Clear your mind of all thoughts and imagine an image such as a clear blue sky. When thoughts pop into your mind, clear them away so your mind is empty. This will be hard to do at first but becomes easier with practice.

This trains your mind to 'see' thoughts rather than just to think them. There are many other benefits to meditation, just find yourself a good basic book or look on YouTube for some guidance if you want more information.

The 80/20 Principle

If you have never read the 80-20 Principle by Richard Koch then I highly recommend you do, it's a great little book. Basically it describes the phenomenon where all things are not equal. In life about 20% of causes are responsible for 80% of results.

What this means to you as a trader is that there are likely a very few things in your trading that are causing most of the problems. By dealing with those few things you will gain a disproportionately better result. So how do you find your biggest trading issue?

Well you probably already know what it is; it is that thing or things that cause you the most frustration. You can probably remember an incident very vividly and painfully caused by this issue. This is where to start. I don't know you personally so I will be covering the different trading behaviours in no particular order.

Just skip ahead so you find the ones that are your biggest problem and start there.

Negative Trading Behaviours

I have grouped typical negative trading behaviours together, that tend to spring from the same cause.

Not Committed to Your System

When a trader is not really committed to their system these are the typical behaviours listed below.

Searching for the Holy Grail trading system that never loses
Buying trading course after trading course
Being too influenced by other traders

This behaviour stems from not having a clear set of criteria when choosing a trading system. The trader just wants to make money and is looking for the magic system that is the RIGHT system for them, ideally a system that never loses and will make them a multi-millionaire in a very short space of time.

Part of the reason for skipping from system to system is a 'grass is always greener 'type of mentality, a fear of missing out by committing to one trading method.

The problem is that years can go by and you will never run out of systems to try. It is time to stop wasting time and find the method that suits you.

If you carry on you can waste years and never get anywhere. It's time to 'turn pro' and commit!

I have already talked about this in Step 1 of this process, however now is the time to repeat the reasons for choosing and sticking to a particular trading system.

It is most important to find a system that is right for your personality and lifestyle. This could be an end of day trading system, a swing trading style, day trading or even scalping. It is the system that when you have tried it felt the most comfortable for you and gave you the greatest success.

If you own a lot of courses already, then it is very likely that you have that system already sitting on your hard drive. There is no point moving on with any of the exercises in this book until you have found the method that works best for you and that you will commit to. When that happens, don't buy any more courses, don't listen to any more traders, stop visiting forums and clear your mind for this trading process.

Trading Too Many of Everything

Behaviours Include

Trading too many strategies
Trading too many time-frames
Trading too many instruments

The other reason for sticking to one system, which beginner traders completely underestimate, is the amount of complexity inherent in even the simplest system. Entry patterns for example are always slightly different from each other, even if it looks the same, there may be different circumstances that led to this type of entry. Why is this important? Well you may find in your records that taking a particular entry in one set of conditions gives you a better result, in which case you may risk less on the entry taken in the other type of condition.

It is these levels of complexity within a system that make the difference as to the level of profitability of the system. It is impossible to master these levels of complexity if you are trading too many systems, time frames and instruments. You need to focus on one trading system, and if necessary one instrument and time frame so you can master the different levels of complexity inherent in that system.

When a trader tries to do too much, he will experience trading as a sense of overwhelm.

They are doing too much and can't focus because their brain is not able to deal with the amount of information. So why do traders do this?

It is a belief about trading that is a sense of lack; they believe that more is better. If one system can make you money then three systems can make you more.

If one time-frame makes money then combining swing trading with scalping will make much more money.

If you can make money trading the forex major pairs, then surely you can make more by trading the crosses, the exotics, indices, stocks and commodities.

You see where I'm going with this....

Look at this image..

This is a photo of Deutsche Bank trading room.

If a trader could handle multiple instruments, and strategies then why do banks have these huge trading rooms? Each of these traders has a small area of responsibility. They only trade as much as they can handle!

You should only trade as much as you can EASILY handle.

There is a trader I know who makes huge money and only swing trades the EUR/USD.

Many pro traders do this. They stick to one pair, one method, and one time frame. The other reason for this is because their brain is not overwhelmed with information they can really focus on their chosen currency pair and become expert on all its moves.

Not all strategies work with all pairs; even if you just trade one strategy with multiple pairs, (which is easily done with an end of day strategy) you will find that the strategy works better with a few pairs. During the process of Kaizen you will then automatically restrict yourself to those few pairs in order to increase your win loss ratio.

Entering Trades Too Early

Entering a trade too early is related to two things, one is a sense of lack about the markets.

The thinking goes something like this. "If I don't get in now price will run away and I will miss this trade. There are only a few trades. What the hell just get in!"

The problem with type of thought process is that it is experienced as a sense of extreme urgency and the trader fails to recognize his thought process because it is happening so fast.

The trader then enters the market and often loses because the market is not ready to move yet. The problem then compounds itself because after a couple of these types of entries, the trader may become so disillusioned about the trade that they fail to enter when the decisive move begins.

This leads to the type of thinking that goes something like this. 'I'll never succeed in trading look at that trade I missed, I'm useless at it' this leads to a sense of failure which can then lead to depression.

This type of behaviour can repeat itself over and over unless the trader changes the way they deal with the problem.

The Physical Method

The way to deal with this problem is two-fold, firstly you deal with the physical behaviours and at the same time you deal with the emotional feelings.

Dealing with the physical side of things means that in a very conscious manner you put physical obstacles in your way so that it becomes a lot more difficult to self-sabotage.

If you normally rush to the charts when an alert goes off, or if you are watching the charts when a trade entry sets up, then you deliberately step away from the charts.

Now this is going to feel uncomfortable, because everything inside you will be screaming to take the entry. However this is the time when you want to slow things down. Have your written entry conditions on a piece of card and take that card and read it over carefully, away from the charts. This will confirm that you are right for taking that extra time and make sure you are not missing anything.

While you are doing this take deep breaths and do the emotional exercises listed below in order to calm yourself.

When you feel calm and you are sure in your mind what you are looking for as an entry point, you can return to check the screen.

Now if you are trading with the longer time frames, it might take hours or even days for the correct entry to show itself. Note the type of behaviours you show in this scenario.

It may be that you have a price alert that goes off long before your actual confirmed entry.

However your behaviour is such that you start staring at the screen and the infinitesimal moves of the market and then you talk yourself into entering before the actual confirmation.

In this type of scenario you need to force yourself to check the screen rather than watch the screen. This type of forced checking can also be used with the lower time frames.

Let's say you need to enter on the close of the 4 hour candle, the price alert has gone off, but instead of checking the screen you check your watch. You then see that there is 2 hours to go before the close of the next four hour candle. (If this is a short term trade, this could be a 15 minute candle)

You find something to do away from the screen, making sure that however much that sense of urgency impels you to open the charts you are deliberately ignoring it and taking control of your actions, at the same time you do the emotional exercises.

Set a time alarm if necessary, and return to the screen at the close of the candle. When you look at the charts have your entry criteria to hand so you can physically check if your entry criteria is met.

This helps with the urge to enter as if you can physically see that your criteria is not met by written evidence it will be harder for your mind to rationalize.

Be mentally prepared for checking rather than watching. Checking means a quick look and check to see if your entry criteria are met, if not met, close the charts and set your alerts until the close of the next candle.

You need to avoid watching the charts at these times because the urgency to enter the market can become overwhelming and will lead to loss of control.

By deliberately structuring your physical actions so that you spend as little time as possible in front of the charts you are building a set of habits that will protect you from self-sabotage. These habits will feel strange at first but after a few times of implementing this new process it will just become a part of your trading routine.

The Emotional Method

The tool I use for this is known as EFT short for emotional freedom technique. This technique was developed by a man called Gary Craig some years back and is the most powerful method I know for reducing the impact of powerful emotions sometimes in a matter of a few minutes. The other virtue of this method is that it extremely simple to do and can be done by anyone.

To give you an idea of the power of this method I am including a link to a video of some EFT therapists using EFT with soldiers with Post Traumatic Stress Disorder. These soldiers had suffered with this disorder since the Vietnam war and more than 20 years later traditional psychotherapy had done very little to help.

Here is the link below. I suggest you take a few minutes to watch this YouTube video to see what I mean, before continuing with the book.

http://tinyurl.com/war-veterans

You can see from the video that even psychiatrists and psychologists admit the power of using EFT to reduce harmful emotions. By combining the power of EFT with behavioral modification in your trading you will see considerable improvements in both your behaviour and the emotional pulls that cause it.

EFT is also used by top sportsmen and women to control their psychology and improve their performance, below is a link to a video showing finger tapping being used by a top formula one driver.

http://tinyurl.com/racing-driver

How to Do EFT

EFT is easy to do; you simply tap yourself lightly with your first two fingers on some specific acupuncture points. While you are tapping you are focusing on the thing that is giving you pain and repeating it out loud. The way you measure improvement is to give the emotion a number between 1-10 and measure after each round of tapping how far the emotions have reduced.

The specific acupuncture points are
The karate chop, at the side of the hand
The inside tip of the eyebrow
The side of the eye
Under the eye
Under the nose
Under the mouth
The collar bone

Under the arm pit (known as the sore spot because you zero in on the slightly painful area)
I am including a link to a YouTube video that shows you the basics visually which makes it much easier to see exactly where these places are and how to tap.

http://tinyurl.com/eft-basics-video

You will see in the video that you use a phrase while you tap that describes the problem. In the video the problem is a 'squeezing pain in my head' which is a physical problem. EFT can be used to help with physical problems as well as emotional ones.
When you tap for your trading issues you need to find a phrase that most closely describes these issues for you. You can replace the

words I use with those of your own that more closely describe your feelings.

Now let's get back to the first problem, entering a trade too early and dealing with the sense of urgency that makes us want to enter the trade too early.

Here is the EFT tapping protocol remember you can substitute words that more closely describe the emotions you feel. This protocol should be done when you are feeling the emotion of urgency to enter a trade.

The best way to summon up the emotions is to actually be in the situation while you are doing it.

The other way is to run a mental movie in your mind that reproduces a specific event where you felt this high level of urgency. As you run the movie, when you get to the part where you feel this high sense of urgency try and build it up to as high a level as possible to most closely represent what you felt during an actual trade. When you feel this heightened emotion give it a number and then do this round of tapping.

EFT Round One
While tapping the karate point repeat 3 times.
Even though I feel such a strong sense of urgency to enter a trade too early I deeply and completely love and accept myself.
Even though I feel such a strong sense of urgency to enter a trade too early I deeply and completely love and accept myself.
Even though I feel such a strong sense of urgency to enter a trade too early I deeply and completely love and accept myself.
Lightly tapping the eyebrow point about 7 times while saying
I need to enter the trade right now even though it's not the right time.
Tap the side of the eye about 7 times while saying
I mustn't miss this trade, it may get away and I will lose out.
Tap underneath the eye about 7 times
I have to enter the trade right now to make myself feel better.
Tap under the nose about 7 times
I feel such a strong feeling that it is really vital that I enter the trade right now.
Tap under the mouth above the chin about 7 times

I know I shouldn't enter this trade too early but I feel that I need to.

Tap just under the collar bone about 7 times

I have to enter the trade to make myself feel better and I don't want to lose out, maybe I'll never get this chance again.

Tap under the arm pit where it feels a bit sore about 7 times

I want to enter the trade, I may lose this chance forever and never make a living trading

(Notice that in the EFT round I also added the thoughts that I had around this issue.)

When you have finished the first round of tapping take your emotional temperature and see if you are still at a high figure when you replay that event in your mind. Repeat the tapping round until you feel that your emotional temperature has reduced to about 1 or zero. You should feel there is no sense of urgency to enter the charts and that in fact you have plenty of time.

You should also have had a paradigm shift so that you simply think differently about the issue. You may now find that you think that there is no point entering a trade unless you can do a low risk entry and if the price moves too fast and you miss the entry then you will look for an opportunity later in the move to enter.

When you have this type of paradigm shift and you feel no sense of urgency to enter the charts too early then test it out on a real trade.

You may find that the sense of urgency re-emerges because of the different situation. Simply do your rounds of tapping in the same way using phrases that most exactly describe what you are feeling. You should combine this tapping with the physical actions you are taking to remove yourself from the charts into another place.

The other thing that may happen while you are tapping is that while this issue fades, other issues start to emerge. You may have a memory or a thought that relates to a feeling of lack or missing out. Maybe you lived in a household where your parents were always worried about money and you have a specific memory related to a parent.

Firstly before tapping on this next issue make sure you have completely cleared the issue you are working on.

Then you can do another round of tapping related to the sense of lack in your life and the specific family memory that popped up.

Example

Even though my dad said 'we are poor and we'll always be poor' I completely love and accept myself.

The important thing to remember is that even if you feel you are not doing it 'right' EFT is very forgiving and you will get results.

So to recap, we find the issues that are having the most negative impact on our trading. We design a set of physical behaviors that will make it difficult to self-sabotage. We integrate those behaviors into a trading routine. We perform this trading routine even though it may feel a bit strange. We use strategies like checking and timing the candles instead of watching the charts. We can also use text price alerts where we set price alerts at just past the break out area so we don't even touch the charts until after a breakout. You can design your own set of trading behaviours that do the job, anything that makes it physically difficult to self-sabotage is fine.

We also use EFT to deal with the emotional issues and neutralize them so we have a different paradigm and no longer wish to repeat this negative behaviour.

Entering Trades Too Late

Here we have the issue of watching trades run away from us. This is the downside of too much analysis and a tremendous fear of being wrong about the trade. Over-analysis is when the trading conditions are all met, the setup and the entry conditions are met and yet the traders mind is still looking for further proof that he is right. They have not really accepted the unknown nature of the 'hard right edge of the charts.'

When there is too much fear attached to the outcome of the trade it usually comes after a series of losses. Now if the trader has been sticking to their proven method then the consequences of this type of losing streak are that it could end at any time. A logical way of dealing with this issue is to measure the longest recorded series of losses for that system and when a loss takes place mentally accept that it may be the beginning of a string of losses equivalent to the longest recorded losing streak.

There is a trader I know who takes a break from trading if they have three losses in a row. They know if that happens something is off with their trading and this removal from the trading arena has saved their account.

However there are also losses which are the normal part of a trading system and the trader needs to be able to deal with them.

One of the issues of too much analysis is attaching the outcome of any particular trade to the imagined long-term outcome of failing in the markets. For example, the traders mind could be telling them,

'If I lose this trade it shows I shouldn't be trading the markets, I am no good at trading, and how am I going to tell my wife? I haven't earned money this month, I'll have to give up trading and get a job, how can I get a job at my age? We'll lose the house and be out on the street and then my wife will leave me; I will end up a bum living on the streets.'

Is it any wonder that with this type of thought process a trader can be frozen with fear?

Thus a reluctance to enter the markets leads to late entries into trades, which leads to losses. It also leads to talking oneself out of trades which should be taken, leading to missed winners. This leads to skewing the normal statistics of the trading system which can turn a winning system into a losing system. This then leads to extreme fear when entering the markets which can lead to a frozen trigger finger where a trader is emotionally and physically unable to enter a trade.

How to Deal with Over-Analysis, the Physical Method

This involves the trader creating a sequence of events and sticking to the sequence without much thought. To reduce the anxiety it helps to reduce the position size of the trade.

On a piece of card write a list of the steps of the trade with little tick boxes next to each step. The goal of the trader is to complete the steps on the card. This way trader only has to focus on each little step at a time and manage the fear of each little part which makes it much less overwhelming.

This changes the goals from results goals like winning the next trade which is out of the traders control to completing each trading step and ticking each box which are process goals. This can give the trader a much needed sense of achievement and get them back on track.

By trading as they should be trading they are more likely to win trades, by winning trades they feel a sense of achievement which encourages them to continue with the correct trading behaviors.

In this physical method the adherence to the tick boxes are designed to override the trader's feelings of fear and tendency to over analyse the trades.

However the use of the emotional method is what causes the trader to have a paradigm shift which makes the steps much easier. We will cover that next.

The Emotional Method

When using the EFT rounds below, create a mental movie of a specific incident in your mind. This movie should take about 30 seconds to one minute going through the whole of the trading sequence.

The emotional crescendo of this mental movie is where you find yourself unable to enter the trade and watching the trade run away from you. Measure the emotions from 1-10, you want them as high as possible and then check on the level with each round of tapping.

You will know you have succeeded when the level is down to 0 or 1 when you are replaying the mental movie in your head. You should also have a paradigm shift where your thoughts about the issue change. You may think something along the lines of

'I don't know what the results of the trade will be, that's not my job. I know the system works over time my job is just to take each trade to the best of my ability'. This will show that you have had a complete change of beliefs around the issue.

You may find that the fears resurface when it's time to enter a real trade, just tap as you did during the practice session. Even if you miss this trade while tapping, by the next trade you should find the issue is resolved.

You may also find that while tapping for this issue, other memories and thoughts arise that are connected to the issue that need dealing with. Make sure you have resolved this particular issue before you go on to the next. The type of thing that could come up would be a foundational one such as memories of a parent saying something like.

'that's too risky we don't take risks with our money' or memories such as parents talking about financial issues with a lot of fear.'

The Emotional Method for Analysis-Paralysis and the Fear of Being Wrong

Remember you can input your own phrase that most closely describes the issue

While tapping the karate point repeat 3 times.
Even though I feel so much fear before I enter a trade I deeply and completely love and accept myself.
Even though I feel so much fear before I enter a trade I deeply and completely love and accept myself.
Even though I feel so much fear before I enter a trade I deeply and completely love and accept myself.
Lightly tapping the eyebrow point about 7 times while saying
I'm too scared to enter the trade I need to know what is going to happen
Tap the side of the eye about 7 times while saying
I need more time to think about this trade, I wish I knew what would happen
Tap underneath the eye about 7 times
I want to see into the future with this trade will it be a winner
Tap under the nose about 7 times
If this trade loses then it means I am a rubbish trader and I can't provide for my family
Tap under the mouth above the chin about 7 times
This trade must be a winner but I am so scared in case it loses

Tap just under the collar bone about 7 times
I can't risk losing this trade, if it loses it means I am a loser who can't provide
Tap under the arm pit where it feels a bit sore about 7 times
I want to wait before I enter the trade until I know for sure it will win

As you can see in the above EFT round I put in the thoughts around the issue of not entering the trade.

By articulating the thoughts out loud it also helps the trader to logically as well as emotionally process their irrationality. It is also very common for other issues to come up such as fear of not being able to provide.

If these thoughts flash into your mind while tapping, then clear the issue you are working on and then work on the 'fear of not being able to provide ' or other issues.

Frozen Trigger Finger 'Can't Take the Trade'

Sometimes the fear of entering the trade has grown so strong that it has become a full-fledged phobia and the trader is literally unable to enter the trade.

With this situation the physical method does not work, what is needed is emotional work to destroy the phobia.

I would advise calling in a professional who specializes in phobia cures and ideally understands the trading environment. However, if you are stuck and you want to have a go yourself then try these methods below.

The NLP Phobia Cure

Find a quiet place to be by yourself while you do this exercise.

Imagine you are sitting by yourself in a movie theatre with a huge movie screen in front of you and the projector behind and above you where a projectionist would normally sit.

Then in your mind's eye see yourself float out of your seat and into the projectionist's booth where you can see yourself sitting in the movie theatre.

You then watch yourself watching a movie describing the sequence of events which led up to you being unable to pull the trigger on the trade.

Watch the movie through in your mind's eye; this should take no longer than 30 seconds to a minute.

Then rewind the film very fast back to the beginning and play it again. Do this three times.

Then play the movie again but instead of the movie being silent this time add in your imagination some very fast and cheerful music like circus music or anything you like.

Then play the movie again but this time if the movie was in color change it to black and white, turn it upside down and play it still with the happy music.

All this time this should be done while you are watching yourself, watching the screen.

This exercise is designed to scramble this series of events in your mind so it doesn't have the same emotional impact. Wait for a few minutes after doing this exercise and then run through the movie where you froze when it came to taking the entry again and see if the intensity of the emotion has lifted.

The EFT Phobia Cure

Before doing this exercise measure the level of intensity you feel when visualizing yourself entering a trade. Run the mental movie again in your head. When you reach the emotional crescendo part of the movie where you are about to enter a trade, keep doing tapping rounds until the intensity has reduced. Repeat until all intensity has gone and you have had a paradigm shift where you think differently about entering a trade. For example you may find yourself thinking, 'entering a trade is just the risk you have to take in trading, you just do the best you can'.

Then test it on a real trade, keep tapping while you are waiting for the entry until you have reduced the fear around entering the trade.

At this point let me relate a warning story of what happened to me when I did this exercise, I completely removed my fear of entering a trade, to the point where I had the opposite problem of entering trades too boldly. If this issue arises after you have cured your fear then you must tap on the issue of entering trades incautiously. You need caution followed by boldness only when you know the trade is right!

I must emphasize that my advice is to see a professional EFT therapist, after all it is your career at stake and you would likely only need one or two sessions to resolve the issue.

See below a link to a YouTube video of an EFT therapist at work curing a phobia in twenty minutes!

http://tinyurl.com/20minphobiacure

Compounding Negative Behaviours in Complete Loss of Control

The next set of behaviours can be grouped together as they represent the same basic cause, a complete loss of control. The problem is one of compounding where if you lose control at the beginning of the trade, that loss of control tends to compound and other behaviours come into play.

Trading outside the strategy
Forcing trades, talking yourself into taking a trade that doesn't exist
Trading without a stop loss
Moving the stop loss further away
Risking too much on a trade
Revenge trading trying to get back at the markets
Closing the trade too early, not allowing it to play itself out.

For example, you are impatient for a trade, so you force a trade, entering in the markets when there is no real trade to take. When the trade moves against you, you move your stop loss further away. The loss compounds and when you finally exit the market you have lost a good portion of your account. In a rage at the markets you have a 'don't care attitude' and start risking too much on trades that don't exist and taking imaginary revenge against the market.

You start trading without stops and next thing you know you are margined out, all because you lost control and got impatient for a trade.

The problem here is that human beings are not wired to maintain self-control for long periods of time.

If you are day trading and staring at the charts for over 2 hours you are quite likely to start losing your self-control. Some traders lose self-control trading hourly charts, some even higher time frames.

If you are wired to be a short term day trader but you start giving back money to the market after 2 hours then only trade for an hour and a half.

Don't trade until you get exhausted, stop while you still have a reasonable degree of mental energy.

One of the biggest ways to increase your level of self-control is to increase the time frames you trade.

If you switch to trading end of day charts then you are unlikely to lose control because too much time is involved.

You check your charts at the end of the trading day, you have ample time to do your research, and there is generally no need to worry about news announcements. When you enter a trade you know that you can't see any results until the following day so it is much easier to close the trading platform and go to bed.

The point I am making is that if you find yourself regularly losing control in the markets then you very likely need to switch to a higher time frame.

If you feel resistance to this change then there is a belief about making money in the markets that is causing a conflict. It is common for traders to believe that the more they trade the more money they will make. They also believe that the harder they work the more they earn. These beliefs are related to how most people earn money, via a job and can lead to over trading and reluctance to move up in time frames where there are less trading opportunities.

Logically they may know they will make more money trading higher time frames but emotionally they feel drawn to scalping and day trading even though those time frames cause them to lose control and their money.

Before we go on to the tapping round for dealing with these beliefs let's take a logical look at the belief that you can make more money by day trading or scalping than by trading the longer time frames.

Firstly let me ask why you got into trading in the first place, was it just to make money or was it to increase your quality of life. When you see rows of bank traders chained to their desks, does that look like quality of life? Those traders burn out very fast because of the high stress environment.

In order to make money in the markets you need to be profitable, if you keep losing control in the markets you can't be profitable. It doesn't matter that you may know a scalper or day trader making thousands a day. If that is not how you are wired to trade the markets then what makes them money could lose all your money. You are better off to give them your money to trade while you go off and do something else.

When you find a method that gives you the lifestyle you want and is a fit for your personality, then you are much more likely to make money. That method includes the time frame that allows you to trade without loss of control.

The Emotional Method

The emotional method for dispelling beliefs that more trading equals more profit in the markets.

Remember you can input your own phrase that most closely describes the issue

While tapping the karate point repeat 3 times.
Even though I believe that I need to take lots of trades to make money in the markets I deeply and completely love and accept myself.
Even though I believe that I need to take lots of trades to make money in the markets I deeply and completely love and accept myself.

Even though I believe that I need to take lots of trades to make money in the markets I deeply and completely love and accept myself.

Lightly tapping the eyebrow point about 7 times while saying

I believe that the harder I work the more money I'll make even though I really know that isn't true.

Tap the side of the eye about 7 times while saying

If I work hard the market will reward me, the harder I work the more reward I'll get

Tap underneath the eye about 7 times

By staying in the market even though I am mentally tired I believe the market will reward me. Hard work always reaps a reward

Tap under the nose about 7 times

If I trade 8 hours a day then I can make big money in trading.

Tap under the mouth above the chin about 7 times

The harder I work the more money I will make

Tap just under the collar bone about 7 times

Taking more trades means I am working hard and hard workers will be rewarded

Tap under the arm pit where it feels a bit sore about 7 times

The more I trade the more I will earn

When you have finished the first round of tapping say out loud to yourself, the harder I work the more money I make and see how true it sound on a scale of 1-10. You should repeat the tapping rounds until that statement doesn't feel true for you anymore.

Wrap Up

Now you know the method for taking back your self-control in the markets.

Where possible create a physical system that makes it difficult to self-sabotage.

Combine this with EFT to reduce emotional intensity, change your beliefs and create a paradigm shift that benefits your trading.

If you want to go on and learn more about EFT there are many good courses you can take. The more you are able to take control of your emotions in trading the better trader you will be.

I hope you found this book helpful, I am always looking for reviews from my readers and as a reward for leaving a review if you email me then I will gladly send you a PDF copy of one of my books of your choice.

I wish you good trading.
LR Thomas

Recommended Resources

Books mentioned in Control Your Inner Trader

The 80 20 Principle by Richard Koch

Outliers by Malcolm Gladwell

The War of Art by Stephen Pressfield

Trading Psychology Video Course

I hope you have found this book a useful resource in your quest to improve your trading performance. If you have enjoyed this book then please leave me a review on Amazon and as a thank you I will send you a PDF copy of this book or a book of your choice.

I love to hear from my readers so if you have any comments or questions, then you can email me at lrthomasauthor@gmail.com.

Trading Mindset Video Course
'Create Your trading Success'
Go to www.traderselfcontrol.com to find out more.

Sign up at my blog http://10XROITradingSystem.com if you would like to learn more about my High ROI Trading Systems.

You can find my video courses here..

http://10xroitradingsystem.com/video-courses/

You can find all my e-books on my Amazon author page or this page on my website.

http://10xroitradingsystem.com/the-ebooks

Overcome Your Fear in Trading

by LR Thomas

Trading the financial markets has large potential rewards but also large potential risks.

You must be aware of the risks and be willing to accept them in order to invest in the financial markets. Don't trade with money you can't afford to lose. No representation is made that any account is likely to or will achieve profits or losses similar to any information found in this book. The past performance of any trading system or methodology does not necessarily indicate future results.

Table of Contents

Books by LR Thomas

Overcome Your Fear in Trading
Control Your Inner Trader
How to Stop Over-trading
The 10XROI Trading System
The Trade Around Your Job System
The High ROI Scalping System
The High ROI End of Day System
Pyramid Your Trades to Profit
Learn to Trade Forex Without Losing Your Shirt

Overcoming Your Fears In Trading

Fear is the most debilitating emotion you can feel and can easily derail your trading career and prevent you taking the necessary steps to become a profitable trader. This book is a practical book unlike many other trading psychology books, it is designed to deal with the problem of fear in trading, not just to describe the problem. It is also a short book because it is designed to solve the problems of fear not to fill up two hundred pages in order to justify a high price!

What qualifies me to write this book? I have been a trader for more than eight years and I am also a qualified therapist trained in hypnosis, NLP and EFT with an interest in behavioural economics and psychology. I have also successfully dealt with my own fear in trading and written a highly regarded trading psychology book 'Control Your Inner Trader'.

Crippling fear can stop any trader, even professional traders from reaching their full potential by striking at the very moment that a trader should be bold.

Fear stops traders entering trades they should be taking
Fear stops traders exiting trades that have moved strongly against them
Fear causes traders to make excuses to themselves so they can avoid the charts, resulting in missed opportunities
Fear causes a trader to hyper-focus on the charts and miss important information that seems obvious after the trade is over.
Fear stops profitable traders increasing their position size when it makes sense to do so.

Fear can strike during a trade when an unexpected event occurs, causing the trader to freeze.

Fear of loss causes a trader to take profits too early.

Fear causes a trader to exit their position before a trade has had a chance to get moving, they talk themselves out of the trade.

Fear of failure can cause system hopping because a trader puts off committing to a system due to their fear that they won't succeed as a trader.

Fear of success can cause a profitable trader to unconsciously sabotage themselves.

Fear of pulling the trigger causes some traders to be physically and emotionally unable to enter a trade, they have developed a full blown phobia.

I wrote this book to help fellow traders identify how this emotion may be affecting their trading, and then to cure themselves of fear in trading forever. Fear is an emotion that can be hidden below our conscious awareness and called by other names such as anxiety, stress and worry.

There are two goals that I have with this book, the first is that you should be able to look at your fear in a different light so that it doesn't stand in the way of executing your trading methodology the way it was meant to be executed.

The second goal is to where possible, remove your fear completely, the exercises in the second half of this book are specifically to remove fear from the trading process.

Either way if you have a new way of thinking about losses as well as the ability to remove fear, you will have a completely different relationship with the fear, and it will be at the very least, a much reduced issue in your trading.

Why Do We Feel Fear?

Why do we feel fear while trading anyway? after all trading is only really pushing some buttons to enter a trade and then more buttons to exit. The problem is that for most traders there is more riding on the results of the trade than mere profit or loss, intertwined with each trade are their fears and hopes for the future!

Imagine that you had hired someone to trade for you. They had their instructions that when a specific event occurs let's say a trend line break they should enter the trade using one per cent of the trading account. They should place a stop loss behind the trend line and a take profit where the trend line began. You teach this person how to do this over a few days and they are paid a weekly wage to take the trades according to the criteria you have given them.

What emotions about the act of trading would your new employee be likely to feel? Well, they may be anxious in case they missed a trade and lost their job. Their fear would be based around making sure they were at the charts for the trigger event, the trend line break, in order to take the trade. After they had entered, they would likely breathe a sigh of relief that they were now in the trade and had placed their stop loss and take profit. They would go on with other things happy now their job was secure and they had performed a task well.

Contrast this with a trader who works full time and fantasizes about becoming a trader to leave behind their boss who is always criticizing them and threatening them with dismissal.

He invents a very simple system of trading; the same system the employee was paid to follow. The system is to enter on a confirmed trend line break putting the stop loss behind the trend line and the take profit at the beginning of where the trend line started. He has thoroughly back tested the system and knows that over time it is profitable.

His plan is to build up his trading account to a point where he can have enough confidence to leave his job. He imagines how he will do this with visions of giving his boss the finger as he turns and walks out of the door, running through his brain.

A trade now sets up and he is at the charts ready to enter the trade. Unknown to him below his conscious thinking he is imagining what his life will be like when he is able to leave his job. He enters the trade, a sudden news announcement spikes price up towards his stop loss, he is vigilant and his fear causes him to close the trade for a small loss. Then price reverses and moves strongly in the original direction. If he had just left the trade alone he would be in profit.

As the trader despairingly watches price run away from him towards his take profit he mentally kicks himself, and his dream of leaving his job and giving his boss the finger becomes less real to him. He has visions of failing at trading and never being able to leave his job, he starts to believe that becoming a profitable trader is less a goal and more of a pipe dream.

He mentally vows that the next time a trade sets up he will stay in the trade and not exit before the trade has a chance to get going. Unfortunately, he gets stopped out on a new spike and his trade turns to a loss. Despairing the trader thinks to himself that the trend line break system must be flawed, what he needs to do is find a system where these type of things don't happen. Off he goes on the search for the trading Holy Grail, searching for the trading system that never loses and will enable him to fulfil his dream of leaving his job.

Although it may not seem obvious at first both of these traders had the same kind of thinking when it came to taking the trade, 'Results Thinking'.

In the first trader however their adherence to the process of trading meant they got paid and so their reward was linked to sticking to the process of trading. Thus their concern was to execute the trade properly and make sure they didn't miss any trades. In their case Results thinking worked very well for their trading.

In the second example Results thinking worked against the trader, they mentally linked the imagined results of their trading 'leaving the job' to the process of trading 'taking the trade' When the trade started to move against them they couldn't see the trade in context, what they could see was their dream evaporating . This caused anxiety or 'fear' and made them exit the trade early. It would be rationalized during the process however as 'conserving capital' or 'exiting fast'. The trader would dig into everything they have ever learned about trading to find a rationalization for exiting their trade too early.

In real life traders don't get paid for taking the trade, at least they don't think they do, this is why they are more likely to think like the second example than the first.

The problem here is that the trader sees their trade in a vacuum, the results of a trade are directly linked to their life goals. This makes it impossible to execute their trade correctly because their fear of losing their dream causes them to interfere with the trade in a negative way. The trader is unable to recognize this and they blame the system and it causes them to do something very common in trading, 'system hop'. They are now caught in the common trading phenomenon the search for the trading Holy Grail.

Reframing the Problem

In NLP or Neuro-Linguistic-Programming there is a therapeutic technique known as re-framing. The idea behind it is that by re-framing the problem the patient sees it differently and their response changes. Let me re-frame this trading issue of seeing trades in a vacuum by telling you a little story.

Years ago I used to be in telephone sales; I sold advertising over the phone and was very good at it. I started off selling low price listings which required us to make calls all day long. We had a target of two sales a day. I copied another top sales person who did not put the phone down the whole day and made a huge amount of money and I believe she still does to this day. I then moved over to another department where the sales were no longer a few hundred pounds but a few thousand pounds. Here people did not seem to work very hard, they spent a lot more time chatting and drinking coffee than picking up the phone. However I moved over to this department with the PROCESS of selling listings and stayed on the phone all day making calls. I started to make a lot of sales even though I wasn't at all experienced in this type of selling and quickly moved up to management where I had to train new sales people how to sell.

What I did was to transfer my process to new sales people by creating a form which had goals for each call and tick boxes for reaching each goal.

One goal would be reach the owner, the next goal would be to get though the script, the next goal would be to answer objection one, then objection two and so on, right up until closing the sale. The goal was to get to three closes.

My trainees were taught to focus on the process of selling and measure their progress by how far they got in the conversation not by how many sales they made. This completely overcame a very common problem in sales of call reluctance and the new sales people could start measuring their achievements by improvements in their performance and not their results.

My training was highly successful and I became able to take an office of completely new trainees who had never sold before and by plugging them into the process of selling rather than just focusing on the results, 'sales', I could get a sales office up and running within two weeks, with sales coming in within a few days.

So how does this story translate to trading?
Supposing your trading performance was completely de-linked from the results of trading and you measured your success by how well you stuck to the process.

Good pre-trade analysis / check
Waiting for price level to be hit/check
Waiting for an entry /check
Taking the entry/check
Waiting until price moved to a point where you can move to break-even/check
Putting in your take profit/check, etc.
This process would be adapted to whatever steps were involved in your trading system.

Your goal would not be to be a profitable or winning trader which is a goal outside your control, your goal would be to be a great trader which would by default make you a profitable trader and which is totally within your control.

Your goal would not be to get winning trades which is completely outside your control; your goal would be to stick to each step of the process, which is totally within your control.

Whatever the win or lose results of the trades were, your trading performance results, that is sticking to the steps and ticking the check boxes would be the source of your achievement.

How would this impact your fear? Well a big part of the fear in trading is due to events outside our control, losses. If you switch to measuring achievement on actions rather than results you are now in the realm of personal control rather than loss of control and as a result you are a lot less likely to fear the results of any particular trade. Just like in selling the sales person is unable to control which call will result in a sale, they just give each call the best performance they are capable of and by default they will become a profitable sales person.

How to Assign Value to Trades

Let me give you another analogy using the sales process. In selling once you know your conversion rates you can assign a value to each call regardless of whether that call results in a sale. Let's say with a new person their conversion ratio was one percent, in other words they had to make a hundred calls in order to make a sale. Let's also say that the commission on a sale was $300, $300 divided by one hundred calls means their call value was $3 per call. They earned $3 per call whether that call resulted in a sale or not. That means that the sales person earned $3 for each of the 99 calls that did not result in a sale. This is a common way of thinking amongst sales people, it helps them to with-stand rejection as they know that it is the rejection that will allow them to get to the 'yes' which gives a monetary value to every call it takes to get to that sale.

As the sales person improves their statistics change, let's say their statistics go from 1% to 5% , they now know that for every 100 calls they make they earn $1500 which means that each call is now worth $15.00

OK so now let's apply this thinking to trading. Let's say when you start out using a particular system you are not very skilled and your win loss ratio is 15% you lose 5 out of 6 trades. When you win a trade you make 10% on your account and when you lose a trade you lose 2% on your account.

This gives an average value to each trade of zero.

You take a sample size of the trades and you analyse them thoroughly looking for a pattern that would enable you to improve your performance, you find that the reason you are only winning 15% of trades is that you enter the trade too early and if you had waited for a confirmed break your win ratio would have been much higher at 30%.

You implement this change and low and behold your win rate goes up, you now win two trades out of six still making 10% on the wins and losing 2% on the losses. You now make 12% on a series of six trades instead of zero percent. Your trade value has now increased from zero to 2%. Every trade is now worth 2% on your account. With every six trades you analyse the results to find ways to make each trade more profitable, you find that your short trades have a higher win ratio than your long trades, you leave the long trades and now only trade shorts.

Your win loss ratio has now increased to three wins in every six with an average value of 4% to each trade whether a winner or loser. Can you get rich with an average 4% value to each trade? You certainly can!

Now is this a simplification? yes of course, you won't have exactly three wins out of every six just like good sales people don't have exactly five sales out of every hundred calls. They may go for a week without making any sales and in the next hundred calls they get ten sales. This is very common in sales which are why the numbers are averaged out to protect the emotional well-being of sales people going through a losing streak.

Going back to trading the reason you only trade a small portion of the account is for the reason that you don't know how long the losing streak will go on for and it's to let the numbers play out so that you can wait for the winners.

So how does this process affect the mind-set of the trader and how can it remove fear? This can help the trader because it enables the trader to focus on the PROCESS of trading and increasing the value of their losing trades, just like having the goal sheet helped new sales people to focus on the PROCESS of selling and increasing the value of their losing calls.

In sales just like trading you have to take a lot of rejection/losses and in order to give your best to the next prospect/trade you need to have a mental paradigm that focuses on process not results. I call this Process thinking and being able to switch over from Results thinking to Process thinking is what will enable a trader to control their fear and trade more consistently.

Process Thinking Versus Results Thinking

In order for a trader to do the necessary work to improve their system and their own trading, they need to see themselves and their system as part of a process. Each part of that process is constantly scrutinized for potential areas of improvement. If you have ever read the book The E-myth by Michael Gerber you will see that the theme of the book is consistency and automation by fine tuning each part of a business process to produce a consistent result.

This is the premise behind a business franchise, a process that can be replicated to provide a consistent experience in different cities or countries. However that franchise may be consistent in the way it operates but that doesn't mean that it has consistent profits. For example a McDonalds in central London has a very different profit level to a McDonalds in a drive through in Blackpool. This is the type of outlook a trader needs to have, they need to focus on improving the quality of their process to a point where if they were able to hand over their entire process to someone who didn't know how to trade, that person would be able to take their process and within a very short training period start trading. This is Process thinking!

Going back to the book The E-myth Michael Gerber describes an experience where he has his hair cut and because he enjoys the experience so much he goes back to the same barber but this time the experience is different, the barber has not given him the same experience he did at his first visit, he did not use hot towels at the end of the shave. This is Results thinking on the part of the barber where they are concerned with the result, giving a shave to a customer not the process which is providing a consistent experience to each customer.

This is why franchises have a much higher success rate than a normal business, because each part of the business is scrutinized to find out the most successful way to execute and then turned into a process. This is the outlook I suggest you apply to your trading, to treat trading as if it were a franchisable business process.

So how does that look in trading? Well we would start off with a working trading methodology that was a rough system just like the trend line break method outlined earlier in the book. We then look to improve every part of our trading process by keeping extensive records and using the concept of a sample size.

Let's say we take a sample size of six trades as we used in the first example at the beginning of this book, we use our first six trades to provide a baseline. The more detailed the number of factors that make up the baseline, the more factors we are able to measure when it comes to improvement.

Let's say we start off with a series of six trades and we have twenty factors that we can measure.

Here are some examples..
Time of day,
Time in the trade,
Entry in to trade
Size stop loss
What factors determine the stop loss
When we moved to break even etc,etc,

We then back test those six trades and see what our results would have been if we had altered one of those factors and used that change in our next sample size and we repeat this using each factor until we get better results.

So what would Process thinking look like for a trader? Well it would be an absolute focus on performance improvement. Results would only be used to gather information about improving performance and the only emotion that should be linked to results is excitement when the data reveals a way of improving trading performance and by default the value of each trade. Since there is always a way to improve performance, that is a constant in trading. Trades are seen in the light of gathering data-sets which is a completely different outlook to trading to win money and change your life.

One of the biggest problems for traders is when they find a profitable system they don't stick to it. However if the focus is on sticking to the plan with the emphasis on trader improvement rather than winning this de-links results or winning, from the trading process. This will give rise to very different emotions in the trader as they will now be able to have a sense of control in their trading. Obviously this Process thinking needs to be applied to a winning system, so the first task of a trader in creating their process is to find a winning system that suits their lifestyle and personality.

This is completely different from the system hopping brought on by the search for the holy grail of trading, a system that never loses. This is a systematic search for a methodology that the trader will be able to adapt and mould to their lifestyle. Before looking for a trading system a traders' criteria should not just be 'making money'.

Criteria should include:
Time available

Patience level (how long can you watch the charts before impulsively entering a trade)

The credibility of the system provider

The simplicity level, the simpler the better.

Back tested results

Forward tested results.

The sooner you can get accurate information on a system the sooner you can commit yourself to a system and use process thinking to become a profitable trader.

Why is Dieting Like Trading?

Let me give you another analogy, why do diets fail? Well diets fail because people can't stick to them but what is it about diets that causes people to fail? The typical dieter is very focused on results, they are looking for fast weight loss and they may even weigh themselves every day. All diet clubs focus on weight loss and the poor member knows that each week they are going to be weighed in front of their fellow members. The problem is that some weeks people who have been sticking to their diet will plateau and not lose any weight or even gain weight, while others will drop pounds seemingly effortlessly. How does that make the dieter feel? They get discouraged and when they get discouraged they start to slip from their diet and next thing you know they are looking for the holy grail of dieting, the next new diet which allows them to lose weight really fast with no deprivation and no plateauing. What they don't realize is that it is the structure of their thinking about the diet that has caused their failure.

Suppose the diet club was different, supposing it focused on acquiring healthy eating habits and adding new habits weekly. Suppose that the records the dieter kept were just related to their performance and completely de-linked from their weight. Well everybody would be on the same playing field; the emphasis would be on the process of weight loss not the results of weight loss. People would focus on the day to day of incorporating new healthier eating habits and exercise habits and by default they would lose weight.

They would ignore plateaus because their results would be seen in perspective. The truth is that no-one can control at what rate they lose weight so to have a weight loss goal which is out of a dieters control is mentally setting the dieter up for failure right at the beginning.

So what is the point to this? It's to demonstrate that different situations that measure performance can in fact be very similar, like selling, dieting and trading. The Results mind set kills performance in all these activities whereas the Process mind set makes it a lot easier to succeed and to trade without negative emotions such as fear.

Now there may be an argument that trading is fundamentally different to other activities like dieting and cold calling because you are risking money and therefore the fear in trading must be greater.

Well cold calling reluctance is rife amongst entrepreneurs, they dread picking up the phone and will find any excuse not to do so, they likely have more fear not less than traders who will usually take a trade even if they feel fearful.
You only have to watch some YouTube videos to know how miserable and frustrated dieters are when they fail at yet another diet. This may partly explain the huge rise in obesity where people lose hope of weight loss and completely give up trying because they believe that 'diets don't work',

How does this relate to fear in trading? Because a trader is unable to control events and yet their dreams of a better life are tied to their trading results, every time they get a negative result in trading it increases their level of fear.

Fear of loss – of their dream
Fear of failure
Fear of losing money
Fear of taking the trade

Fear of missing a trade
Fear of letting the trade play out
Fear of losing their profits etc.

Let's go back to this fear of loss and explore it a bit further is it really about money? If you rent an apartment and pay your rent every month are you terrified to pay your rent because you are losing money, likewise when you pay a bill or a subscription on a service are you fearful of the loss of money?
No of course not, and yet that is money disappearing every month without fail. So if it's not fear of losing money, maybe it is fear of not getting value for your money, after all when you pay money for your rent you are getting value which is a roof over your head. If that is the case then the more value we can assign to a losing trade the less we will fear the loss.

We have already covered assigning a monetary value to a trade earlier on, later in the book I will cover other ways to assign value to losing trades.

The paradigm shift that I am hoping you get from these arguments is that flawed thinking or Results thinking causes fear and distress not only among traders but also amongst dieters and cold callers, any performance based activity where the results are outside a persons' personal control causes fear. The solution for a trader is to lose their Results thinking and move over to PROCESS thinking.

Fear of the Unknown

Let's get back to the problem of fear for traders and look at the issue of fear of the unknown.

Whenever you take a major step in life whatever that step may be you can feel huge amounts of fear. This is why people stay in failing marriages for many years until the pain of staying finally out-weighs the fear of leaving and the person takes action to dissolve the marriage.

In trading every trade is a step into the unknown and therefore each trade can be loaded with fear for those people who crave certainty in their lives. However certainty is only present in physical laws such as gravity and death, in trading the only constant is uncertainty.

So how can a fear of the unknown be dealt with? In my book the 10XROI Trading System, I outline the way I personally dealt with the stress of the unknown in trading. Reducing outcomes!

By having a fixed take profit I immediately reduced the number of outcomes the trade could have. The outcomes were reduced to only three, win 1-10, loss, or break even. There are also fixed rules for placing a stop loss and for moving to break even.

Contrast that with the number of outcomes faced by the normal trader. The stop loss is not selected in a way that leaves no doubt and so when price moves against the position many traders move their stops further away. There is also a lot of fear and doubt when price approaches the stop and often the trader moves the stop closer to reduce the amount they stand to lose.

They have no fixed plan for moving to break even, sometimes they find they move to break even and get stopped out and price then turns against them back in the direction of the original trade, this can cause a trader to not move to break even in the next trade and then watch as price moves in their direction and then reverses against them and stops them out at a loss.

Even if they have a plan for take profit they are looking at price action to determine when to get out. Mostly they will exit the trade early because as price reverses and they see their profits dissipating the fear of loss takes over and they talk themselves into exiting the trade. Alternatively they can stay in the trade too long and watch as their profit disappears while they are mentally kicking themselves for not exiting earlier.

This type of trading means there can be numerous variable trade outcomes and a trader will never know going in what outcome they are going to get. This can produce intense anxiety as every time a trader places a trade it is a leap into the unknown, the unknown area of how they will personally react to events.

There are two ways to deal with this, either emotionally where the trader just accepts that every time they enter a trade they may get very different results from what they intended (which is difficult), or they can structure their trading so that they have a set of rules which have been back tested to provide the most profitable outcome overall and this forms the basis for their trading.

The trader knows that this means that lots of times they will be stopped out early or miss profits they could have got if they had stayed in the trade but the reassurance is in the fact they know that this is the proven most profitable way to manage their trade. This removes a lot of uncertainty from the trading process and is something I highly recommend. In my 10XROI Trading System the stop loss is carefully selected at a strong S/R level so it makes it difficult to justify moving the stop loss. The take profit is a fixed 1-10 ROI which overall has been shown to be the most profitable take profit for this system and there is a fixed rule of moving to break even which is to wait for a large pull back to near the entry and then a continuation in the trade direction. These rules were created in such a way as to provide a level of certainty in an uncertain environment.

So a practical solution for fear of the unknown in trading is to work out what the overall most profitable way of trading the system is and then design the system rules around that. This provides emotional protection against seeing your trades stopped out or going on to make more profits after exit. You know that you have chosen the best set of rules for the system regardless of what happens on any individual trade.

Fear of Failure

This is a big one! Fear of failure is a prevalent fear amongst traders and can become a self-fulfilling prophesy. The trader is so afraid of failing at trading after a series of losses that they start thinking of trading overall in a very negative light. Even while they are still system hopping and trying new systems they lose faith in what they are doing. The problem with this is that when a trader believes that they will fail at trading, this belief then goes on to filter how they interpret the trades. In other words they subconsciously look for trades that will support their belief that they will fail at trading.

This is because they now have a mental filter that they add to their trading system which is a belief in their ultimate failure.

This filter overrides the other mental filter they are assuming which is the system they are trading and makes it impossible to succeed if the trader is unconsciously looking to the charts for proof that they will fail at trading. Let me give you an analogy

The Red Car Bias

Imagine you are driving on the motorway with your family and you decide to have a contest to see who can spot the most red cars in the next ten minutes. The winner will get $100.

What will then happen is that the focus of the passengers will be on spotting red cars. They will probably see more red cars in that short period of time than they have ever seen before, (by seen I mean noticed and paid real attention to). What will happen during this time is that they will mentally tune out the black, blue, green, silver and other colour cars from their consciousness. They will still see these cars but now they will slide under their mental radar because their attention is focused on spotting red cars and so they won't really notice any other vehicle.

This is the same thing a trader does when they are learning a new trading system. They apply a mental filter to the charts and they look at the charts through that filter to find trading opportunities. However when a trader has a secret belief that they will fail in trading they apply a further filter to the charts which ensures that their beliefs will be confirmed, they add a failure filter. How do you know if you are wearing a failure filter and more importantly how can you change that filter to a success filter.

Signs That You May Be Wearing a Fear of Failure Chart Filter.

When you back test the system you get lots more winning trades than you do when you trade the system either demo or live.

You notice good trades after they have finished but fail to see them setting up.

You often miss taking trades that would have been winners

You trade to failure, (this often happens in day trading where the trader will keep taking trades until they have given back all their winnings to the market).

You find yourself taking trades that you later notice went against your system parameters and you find yourself wondering why you ever took the trade.
If you have spent quite a while trying to make a success of trading and trying lots of systems using Results thinking it is very likely that you will have sustained a belief in trading failure. If these type of things are frequently happening then it's pretty certain that you have added a failure filter to your chart analysis.

Fear of failure is an unavoidable result of pinning your hopes on trading as a way of delivering you from some unwanted part of your life such as a full-time job. The would -be trader has a job that they hate for whatever reason and this is how they were attracted to trading in the first place because it allows them the freedom that they don't receive in their job.

The idea of working from your laptop and being location and financially independent is a very appealing one. The problem as I mentioned earlier is that with results thinking each trade is inextricably linked to the traders dream which puts a lot of stress on the trader to get it right. It places a filter on the traders field of vision when they look at the charts which is not a useful one because 'leaving the job' is not a useful addition to a trading arsenal, just a hindrance.

The consequences of failure become that the traders dreams are not realized and this leads to a fear of failure which becomes a self-fulfilling prophesy. The more the trader fears failure and visualizes the unpleasant consequences of failure such as having to stay in their job, the more likely they are to create failure; it's an endless feedback loop.

Imagine that instead of being a trader you wanted to be a photographer, your dream was to leave your job and make a living through your photography. Would every photograph you took be laced with your hopes and dreams and if so what sort of photos would result? Wouldn't the photographer in that moment of taking the photo have to give themselves up to the act of creating the best and most beautiful photo possible in order to create the type of photos that would sell?

Wouldn't the same thing apply to any endeavour? Do you think Tiger Woods became great by mentally imagining what would happen if he didn't win the tournament every time he took a shot? On the contrary, in order to become great he had to assume a self-created mental attitude that mentally dismissed any consequences in order to take the next shot as it should be taken.

When you read about Tiger Woods' upbringing, you will find out that his father employed a lot of mental techniques in his sons' training including a type of self-hypnosis in order to keep Tigers' focus on his performance absolute.

Why do all great athletes have coaches? Not just for their physical performance, it is the mental side of winning that is so important for an athlete to master. If an Olympic athlete trained for years with visions of what their life would be like if they failed dancing before their eyes every time they had an injury or lost a competition, they would never get to the Olympics. After all the odds against an athlete winning the Olympic Gold are far greater than a trader making a living through trading. How do Olympic athletes need to think in order to stand the uncertain future they have mapped out for themselves, it is the same type of mind set that a trader needs to adopt in order to have any chance of trading success. They need to believe thoroughly in their ultimate success in a way that rises above their current results. What tools do athletes use to achieve this? visualization and affirmations. We will cover these later on in the book.

From Failure to Success

So, how do you go about changing the filter from a failure filter to a success filter? Well firstly let's define what a success filter is. A success filter is the polar opposite of a failure filter. Because you have a belief that you will succeed in trading you notice the good trades as they are setting up and mentally delete the bad trades from your awareness (just like in the red car bias). You make sure you are at the chart when the correct trades are forming and you are able to easily catch trades.

The amount of your winning trades tallies with the back tested results of the system.

You easily avoid bad trades; they recede below your notice as you are focusing on trades that are likely to succeed.

So what is a practical way to turn a failure filter into a success filter? This goes back to process thinking and it's about redefining success and failure.

I am also going to bring in something that you may regard as a bit woo-woo... affirmations!

To change your belief about your trading failure you combine process thinking with success affirmations.

This is very different from results thinking because results' thinking assumes you have the power to control your trading results. Process thinking assumes you have the power to control your trading actions and affirmations replace the failure belief with new more powerful success beliefs.

So how do you redefine failure and success in trading, well trading success is not an end goal.

People think about trading success as if it is a destination rather than a journey. There is no point in time that you can say I am a trading success because that can change the next day if your behaviours change or the market changes. Trading is an ongoing journey of increasing excellence; the only thing you can say for sure is that you are becoming an increasingly better trader. How do you become an increasingly better trader? You learn from each mistake and input changes to your trading routines and your trading system to increase your performance.

There are no gold medals for trading success, the only gold medal you can win is the increased size of a trading account and there is no definitive point where you say I have reached perfection, rather you are always striving for perfection while knowing you will never get there.

So how can this redefine success and failure in trading, it means that if you learn from a mistake and adjust your trading to become a better trader then you have succeeded in your quest to achieve trading perfection. Thus the goal is to learn from your mistakes to increase performance. Every mistake you make is looked at with the viewpoint of here is an opportunity to improve your performance not as a sign that you have failed at trading.

Let me tell you another story to see if I can make this clearer, back to my selling days for another trading analogy. Whenever we started a new selling project we would come up with an idea for a product and in order to test whether the product had legs we would write a very rough sales pitch and get on the phone. We fully expected that there would be lots of objections and no's and that was the whole point! We wanted to see what the objections were so we could improve our sales process. Whenever people turned us down we would ask why and get the information we needed. Within a few days we knew whether the project was likely to succeed and also we knew what we needed to do to develop the product and improve our sales pitch.

Those mistakes we made in our initial sales pitch were of great value as they led us to be able to perfect our performance.

The mind-set we adopted was one of Kaizen, which is Japanese for "improvement" or "change for the best" and refers to philosophy or practices that focus upon continuous improvement of processes. Each change in itself may be small, but the compounded effect of many small improvements leads to huge improvements overall.

I go into this into a lot more depth in my book Control Your Inner Trader.

So let's go back to how to redefine success and failure, if the process of trading is one of constant improvement of your performance and a mistake gives you the opportunity to improve your trading performance then that mistake has value. How do you quantify that value? by how easily you are able to implement the changes necessary and by how that change is able to improve your trading performance.

Assigning Value to Each Trade.. Continued

Let's go back to assigning a monetary value to each trade; we worked out that by averaging the value of all our trades each trade could be given a monetary value, a percentage that represented the average value of each trade. Let's say that you are a winning trader and you have assigned a monetary value to your trades of 2%, now you are also going to assign a value to each trade that allows you to improve performance.

So if there is a fixed value assigned to mistakes that allow you to improve performance, let's say the value is 'K', then each trade can be allotted a percentage value, plus or minus K.

If a winning trade enables you to increase performance the trade has the value of 2% plus 'K' or 2K

If a winning trade does not enable you to increase performance then it only has a value of 2.

If a losing trade enables you to increase performance then it has a value of 2% + K or 2K

If a losing trade does not enable you to increase performance then it only has a value of 2.

Now let's take this even further, it makes sense that in order to increase the percentage value of each trade you need information that will allow you to improve your performance. Therefore the more K trades you have the more likely you are able to increase your trade percentage value.

If you have no K trades you can't increase the monetary value of each trade therefore 'K' has a monetary value in so much as it enables you to increase each trade percentage.

So this now lets us look at our trades in a new light, they either give us a chance to increase our average trade percentage or they don't, any trade winner or loser which does not give us this information is by definition less valuable than any trade winner or loser that does give us this information.

As trading is an ongoing quest to achieve excellence then 'K' is an integral part of that journey.

In order to quantify 'K' our process goal is to add an K element to each trade. We want each trade to have a value that goes beyond its monetary value and allows us to improve. This gives us a new way to assess our results and also shows how vital it is to record our results in a way that allows us to improve.

I recently conducted a survey among my trading subscribers to my blog http://10XROITradingSystem.com. Out of the six traders who filled in the survey two traders were profitable. One of those traders kept detailed records and had a trading routine; the other profitable trader said that keeping records was one of his biggest challenges. He understood that not keeping records was a weakness that was preventing him achieving further improvement The other four traders did not keep trading records . This means that 5 out of the six traders surveyed had trades with no 'K' value.

This shows how vital it is to be able to assign an 'K' Value to your trades in order to succeed in your quest for continuous improvement, that is the job of a professional trader.

How does this outlook help with fear, well if all trades have a value that goes beyond the result of the trade then it gives you another way to look at trading besides wins or losses.

If your goal is to be able to assign an K value to each trade then you will keep meticulous notes. You know that you can't improve the percentage of each trade without increasing the number of 'K' trades therefore your goal has now changed from winning a trade which is completely outside your control to improvement of performance which is totally inside your control.

If you adopt this outlook then the correct trading mind set will be more one of curiosity about how you performed, and what is the piece of learning that this next trade will give you.

Even if you are starting off as a losing trader and each trade has a '- percentage' value it should still have a 'K' value. It is only by having a 'K' value that you can increase the percentage of each trade.

Therefore the most important thing about each trade is the 'K' Value!!!!

What I am trying to do here is re-frame the way you look at trading, if you wear Process goggles rather than Results goggles then you will be looking at each trade as a way of getting 'K'.

If you look at trading as a way of getting 'K' then this will remove the fear factor attached to results thinking which is attached to getting winning trades with a monetary value and attaching failure to something which you have no control over .

Process thinking and going for 'K' in each trade is within a traders' control and the percentage value of each trade will increase by default as you implement Kaizen.

Confident Trading

Going back to the survey I carried out with six of my trading subscribers, two of the traders (the profitable ones) replied that they had no confidence in their trading analysis.

Lack of confidence in trading analysis is really another way of saying fear of being wrong.

Well if all trades should have a 'K' value then that now gives a monetary value to being wrong. If there is a monetary value to being wrong which is 'K' (the opportunity to improve future performance) then there is no downside to being wrong, on the contrary there is a huge up-side. Being wrong can make you money and can certainly help prevent losing money.

For example you have probably read stories of traders who blew out their accounts, it only took a few times for that to happen before the trader learned their lesson, traders don't keep blowing out their accounts, it's too painful, and therefore blowing their accounts had a 'K' value.

With a new process mind-set which is focused on improvement of trading performance then the fear of being wrong will be replaced by a different set of emotions such as curiosity about the new learning you will be able to implement in your trading.

Paradigm Shifts Cure Fear

The purpose of the previous chapter was to engineer a paradigm shift in your thinking. The paradigm shift that all trades should have value that goes beyond the monetary and that the way to increase the trade % value is by default and it happens as a result of the 'K' value provided by trades that will help in the process of Kaizen. You now know that becoming a successful trader is not a one off event but a life long journey and so you can take a longer term view.

Hopefully by fully accepting this new paradigm of your trading results you will change your reaction to trading losses and remove fear from your trading.

Visualisation to Improve Trading

Athletes of all standards routinely use visualisation techniques; it has been proven in numerous studies that mental practice is as good as physical practice for improving athletic performance. How can traders use visualisation to improve their trading and remove fear?

Firstly they can mentally rehearse what to do in case of an unexpected event, for example if a news spike pushes price towards their stop loss, an event that would normally cause the trader to react by moving their stop further away or exiting the trade they can mentally practice the correct reaction over and over until it becomes installed in their physiology. The next time they face the event the default reaction will be the action that has been mentally practised time and again.

They can visualise staying in the trade to their take profit instead of exiting early during a pull-back, mentally going through different scenarios where they see pull-backs and feel the emotion that they would normally feel but staying in the trade instead of exiting.

Traders can use visualisation for trade recognition, mentally going through what different trade set-ups would look like prior to an entry.

Visualisation could be used to resist the urge to enter bad trades, mentally imagining being tempted, but instead of taking a trade , closing the trading platform and walking away, seeing the temptation as a signal that it is time to leave the charts.

Visualisation can be used to imagine yourself as a successful trader, learning from your mistakes and constantly improving your performance, it is used to create your new successful trader identity.

Every bad habit in trading can be erased using mental rehearsal or visualisation and likewise every good habit can be reinforced.

The trader can also use visualisation to help remove fear, by visualising every scenario that would normally cause the trader to feel fear and going through it again and again, using the EFT techniques in the second half of the book. In this way fear can be systematically removed from the trading process.

Affirmations to Instil Success Beliefs

Affirmations are an extremely useful tool to install a success mind-set in a trader. Affirmations can be used to undo the failure filter that a trader may have unconsciously installed after a series of losses and override those failure setting with a new success mind set.

Let me tell you a story of how this worked for me, back in my twenties I was going through a bad patch financially, whatever I did I couldn't seem to make any decent money and I was living on benefits. I was so sick of my situation that when I met a man during that time who told me to do these exercises I took it to heart and used the following affirmation hundreds of times a day.

I AM RICH

I also combined these affirmations with visualisation, I visualised living in a big house in Hampstead (a very expensive area in North London), driving a Mercedes car and sitting on white leather sofas, for some reason white leather sofas symbolised luxury to me.

Within two years I was living in a small house in Hampstead, with cream leather sofas and within three years I was living in a huge house in Bushy with an indoor swimming pool and driving a white Mercedes. The house in Hampstead had been given to myself and my husband as a business perk and I was given the white Mercedes as a company car. I didn't get exactly what I visualised but only because when the time came I was visualising something slightly different. For example I had visualised a sports car but after having children I wanted a family car instead.

The affirmations combined with the visualising techniques attracted what I wanted into my life.

So use affirmations; choose affirmations that are meaningful to you, such as...

I AM A WEALTHY SUCCESSFUL TRADER

Say it to yourself hundreds of times a day without really thinking about it , do it while you are walking or exercising or doing anything that doesn't require you to think.

This will enable this message to slip underneath your conscious awareness in to your unconscious mind and replace your limiting beliefs and failure filter with a success filter. Combine the affirmations with detailed visualisation of the things that you want and the life you want to lead, do it every day as an essential part of your trading routine and notice the results.

Do it even if you don't believe it works, you have nothing to lose but a little effort and everything to gain!

Passion in Trading

Many traders are very passionate about trading and a big part of their dream to leave their job and trade for a living is to do something they are passionate about instead of something they find boring and stressful.

What the trader doesn't realize is that it is very difficult to sustain passion in something when you are financially dependent on it and it is causing a great deal of pain. How long do you think that passion would last if a trader had to depend on trading for their next months' rent? The trader could easily end up hating trading with the same amount of passion that they loved it. The problem with being so passionate about trading is that trading is a profession that requires a huge amount of self-discipline. Unless you are a scalper that takes hundreds of trades a day most of the time is spent waiting for a trade not actually trading. It is not like a video game where the action is continuous. Passion in trading can cause a trader to seek more of the excitement by over trading. Passion and self-discipline are uneasy companions. When a trader starts to become more skilled they may complain that they find trading boring, that is because good trading **IS** boring. Good trading requires a trader to wait for the right moment to take a trade and waiting is a very boring activity.

Therefore the point I am trying to get to is that if the trader wants passion for a profession they should add another activity besides trading. They will find their life a lot easier financially as well as emotionally if they have a number of rewarding activities. The best attitude towards trading in my opinion is one of interest but not passion. Passion should be saved for other activities such as photography or writing or any other hobby that provides intrinsic rewards not linked to monetary gain. The ideal situation in my opinion for a trader who wants to leave their job is to have a number of profit centres of which trading is just one. Let me give you another analogy to demonstrate.

When I was a sales person I would find myself under a lot of stress because one week I would make two or three sales and earn £1200 -1500 and the next week I wouldn't make any thing. After a week or two without selling I would become more stressed until finally I got another cluster of sales but my income was very cyclical. I didn't realize that was the nature of selling until I became a sales manager and started to earn an override on an office of sales people. I then realized that all the sales people were cyclical, some weeks I would earn from one sales person and some weeks from another sales person, but because my income was now from all the sales people it had stabilized .

The great advantage to a job is the stability of the monthly income, the great disadvantage to trading is the instability of the monthly income. However if a trader has a number of different sources of income this can provide a level of financial stability to replace the stability of their job income.

How does stability of income and dividing their attention between a number of different activities impact fear. Well going back to the basics of life like paying the rent, if you have a number of sources of income besides trading which like sales is very cyclical, then you are more likely to have a dispassionate view towards your month to month trading results and particularly to the results of each trade. You need to have this view about trading because the very nature of trading is one of cyclical earnings and a lifelong journey of increasing excellence not a one off event; understanding this enables a trader to keep their trading results in perspective.

This is vital in order to reduce anxiety, if a trader wants to leave their job and trade for a living my advice is to think about how they would be able to create a number of income streams that combined together would mimic the stability of their monthly income from a job.

Exercises to Cure Fear in Trading

In the previous chapters we were focused on changing our trading paradigm to one where we could trade without fear.

The way we do this is by using Process thinking rather than Results thinking , by assigning a monetary value as well as an improvement value to trades and also seeing trades as part of a set or sample size which we will use for research into how to improve our next sample size.

We also understand that trading success is a journey not a destination and that it is dangerous to link our dreams directly to trading as this is likely to make it very difficult to trade successfully.
Now I am going to cover some exercises which deal directly with fear in trading. The first exercise deals specifically with the fear of taking a trade,

I have already covered this in my book Control Your Inner Trader but it is relevant to repeat this exercise here.

The tool I use for this is known as EFT short for emotional freedom technique. This technique was developed by a man called Gary Craig some years back and is the most powerful method I know for reducing the impact of powerful emotions sometimes in a matter of a few minutes. The other virtue of this method is that it extremely simple to do and can be done by anyone.

To give you an idea of the power of this method I am including a link to a video of some EFT therapists using EFT with soldiers with Post Traumatic Stress Disorder. These soldiers had suffered with this disorder since the Vietnam war and more than 20 years later traditional psychotherapy had done very little to help.

Here is the link below. I suggest you take a few minutes to watch the video to see what I mean, before continuing with the book.
http://tinyurl.com/war-veterans

You can see from the video that even psychiatrists and psychologists admit the power of using EFT to reduce harmful emotions and make Improvements in both your behaviour, and the emotional pulls that cause it.

How to Do EFT

EFT is easy to do; you simply tap yourself lightly with your first two fingers on some specific acupuncture points. While you are tapping you are focusing on the thing that is giving you pain and repeating it out loud. The way you measure improvement is to give the emotion a number between 1-10 and measure after each round of tapping how far the emotions have reduced.
The specific acupuncture points are

The karate chop, at the side of the hand
The inside tip of the eyebrow
The side of the eye
Under the eye
Under the nose
Under the mouth
The collar bone

Under the arm pit (known as the sore spot because you zero in on the slightly painful area)

I am including a link to a YouTube video that shows you the basics visually which makes it much easier to see exactly where these places are and how to tap.

http://tinyurl.com/eft-basics-video

You will see in the video that you use a phrase while you tap that describes the problem. In the video the problem is a 'squeezing pain in my head' which is a physical problem. EFT can be used to help with physical problems as well as emotional ones.

When you tap for your trading fear issues you need to find a phrase that most closely describes these issues for you. You can replace the words I use with those of your own that more closely describe your feelings.

Fear of Entering a Trade

When using the EFT rounds below, create a mental movie of a specific incident in your mind. This movie should take about 30 seconds to one minute going through the whole of the trading sequence.

The emotional crescendo of this mental movie is where you find yourself unable to enter the trade due to a high level of fear and watching the trade run away from you. Measure the emotions from 1-10, you want them as high as possible and then check on the level with each round of tapping.

You will know you have succeeded when the level is down to 0 or 1 when you are replaying the mental movie in your head. You should also have a paradigm shift where your thoughts about the issue change. You may think something along the lines of

'I don't know what the results of the trade will be, that's not my job. I know the system works over time my job is just to take each trade to the best of my ability'. This will show that you have had a complete change of beliefs around the issue.

You may find that the fears resurface when it's time to enter a real trade, just tap as you did during the practice session. Even if you miss this trade while tapping, by the next trade you should find the issue is resolved.

The other thing that may happen while you are tapping is that while this issue fades, other issues start to emerge. You may have a memory or a thought that relates to a feeling of lack or missing out. Maybe you

96

lived in a household where your parents were always worried about money and you have a specific memory related to a parent.

Firstly before tapping on this next issue make sure you have completely cleared the issue you are working on.

Then you can do another round of tapping related to the sense of lack in your life and the specific family memory that popped up.

Example

Even though my dad said 'we are poor and we'll always be poor' I completely love and accept myself.

The important thing to remember is that even if you feel you are not doing it 'right' EFT is very forgiving and you will get results

The Emotional Method for Analysis-Paralysis and the Fear of Entering a Trade

Remember you can input your own phrase that most closely describes the issue
While tapping the karate point repeat 3 times.
Even though I feel so much fear before I enter a trade I deeply and completely love and accept myself.
Even though I feel so much fear before I enter a trade I deeply and completely love and accept myself.
Even though I feel so much fear before I enter a trade I deeply and completely love and accept myself.
Lightly tapping the eyebrow point about 7 times while saying
I'm too scared to enter the trade I need to know what is going to happen

Tap the side of the eye about 7 times while saying

I need more time to think about this trade, I wish I knew what would happen

Tap underneath the eye about 7 times

I want to see into the future with this trade will it be a winner

Tap under the nose about 7 times

If this trade loses then it means I am a rubbish trader and I can't provide for my family

Tap under the mouth above the chin about 7 times

This trade must be a winner but I am so scared in case it loses

Tap just under the collar bone about 7 times

I can't risk losing this trade, if it loses it means I am a loser who can't provide

Tap under the arm pit where it feels a bit sore about 7 times

I want to wait before I enter the trade until I know for sure it will win

As you can see in the above EFT round I put in the thoughts around the issue of not entering the trade.

By articulating the thoughts out loud it also helps the trader to logically as well as emotionally process their irrationality. It is also very common for other issues to come up such as fear of not being able to provide.

If these thoughts flash into your mind while tapping, then clear the issue you are working on and then work on the 'fear of not being able to provide ' or other issues.

Fear turned into a phobia

Frozen Trigger Finger 'Can't Take the Trade'

Sometimes the fear of entering the trade has grown so strong that it has become a full-fledged phobia and the trader is literally unable to enter the trade.

With this situation the physical method does not work, what is needed is emotional work to destroy the phobia.

I would advise calling in a professional who specializes in phobia cures and ideally understands the trading environment. However if you are stuck and you want to have a go yourself, then try these methods below.

The NLP Phobia Cure

Find a quiet place to be by yourself while you do this exercise. Imagine you are sitting by yourself in a movie theatre with a huge movie screen in front of you and the projector behind and above you where a projectionist would normally sit. Then in your mind's eye see yourself float out of your seat and into the projectionist's booth where you can see yourself sitting in the movie theatre. You then watch yourself watching a movie describing the sequence of events which led up to you being unable to pull the trigger on the trade.

Watch the movie through in your minds' eye; this should take no longer than 30 seconds to a minute.

Then rewind the film very fast back to the beginning and play it again. Do this three times.

Then play the movie again but instead of the movie being silent this time add in your imagination some very fast and cheerful music like circus music or anything you like. Then play the movie again but this time if the movie was in colour change it to black and white, turn it upside down and play it still with the happy music.

All this time this should be done while you are watching yourself, watching the screen.

This exercise is designed to scramble this series of events in your mind so it doesn't have the same emotional impact. Wait for a few minutes after doing this exercise and then run through the movie where you froze when it came to taking the entry again and see if the intensity of the emotion has lifted.

The EFT Phobia Cure

Before doing this exercise measure the level of intensity you feel when visualizing yourself entering a trade. Run the mental movie again in your head. When you reach the emotional crescendo part of the movie where you are about to enter a trade, keep doing tapping rounds until the intensity has reduced. Repeat until all intensity has gone and you have had a paradigm shift where you think differently about entering a trade. For example you may find yourself thinking, 'entering a trade is just the risk you have to take in trading, you just do the best you can'.

Then test it on a real trade, keep tapping while you are waiting for the entry until you have reduced the fear around entering the trade.

At this point let me relate a warning story of what happened to me when I did this exercise, I completely removed my fear of entering a trade, to the point where I had the opposite problem of entering trades too boldly. If this issue arises after you have cured your fear then you must tap on the issue of entering trades incautiously. You need caution followed by boldness only when you know the trade is right!

I must emphasize that my advice is to see a professional EFT therapist, after all it is your career at stake and you would likely only need one or two sessions to resolve the issue.

See below an EFT therapist at work curing a phobia in twenty minutes!
http://tinyurl.com/20minphobiacure

The EFT Method for Belief in Failure

This tapping sequence is to deal with the belief that we will fail in trading which acts as a filter and causes us to take losing trades and mentally delete the winners

Remember you can input your own phrase that most closely describes the issue

While tapping the karate point repeat 3 times.
Even though I believe I will ultimately fail to be a successful and profitable trader I deeply and completely love and accept myself.
Even though I believe I will ultimately fail to be a successful and profitable trader I deeply and completely love and accept myself.
Even though I believe I will ultimately fail to be a successful and profitable trader I deeply and completely love and accept myself.
Lightly tapping the eyebrow point about 7 times while saying
I know I will fail at trading, I've failed before and I will fail again.
Tap the side of the eye about 7 times while saying
It's too difficult to succeed at trading, that's for other people, smarter people than me, I know I will ultimately fail at trading

Tap underneath the eye about 7 times

I will fail at trading I don't know why I bother I believe I will ultimately fail

Tap under the nose about 7 times

I will fail at trading and not be able to provide for myself or my family

Tap under the mouth above the chin about 7 times

I am so scared that I will fail at trading

Tap just under the collar bone about 7 times

I am so frightened that after all this work it will be for nothing and I will fail at trading.

Tap under the arm pit where it feels a bit sore about 7 times

I am a trading failure, I know I will fail.

Fear of Success

This tapping sequence is to deal with the fear that we will succeed in trading which acts as a filter and causes us to take losing trades and mentally delete the winners.

Remember you can input your own phrase that most closely describes the issue

While tapping the karate point repeat 3 times.

Even though I feel so much fear that I will succeed in trading that I sabotage my own success, I deeply and completely love and accept myself.

Even though I feel so much fear that I will succeed in trading that I sabotage my own success, I deeply and completely love and accept myself.

Even though I feel so much fear that I will succeed in trading that I sabotage my own success, I deeply and completely love and accept myself.

Lightly tapping the eyebrow point about 7 times while saying

I'm afraid of success, who am I to be a great trader?

Tap the side of the eye about 7 times while saying

I'm scared that I will succeed in trading and outshine other members of my family

Tap underneath the eye about 7 times

I'm scared I will be rich, rich people are bad people

Tap under the nose about 7 times

I'm scared other people will change their opinion of me if I succeed

Tap under the mouth above the chin about 7 times

I'm scared I will lose my friends and family if I succeed in trading

Tap just under the collar bone about 7 times

Success in trading is not who I am it doesn't feel right

Tap under the arm pit where it feels a bit sore about 7 times

I am scared to succeed in trading; it means I love money too much

Fear of Fear

This tapping sequence is to deal with fear of feeling fear during trading and the fear we won't be able to cope with the fear.

Remember you can input your own phrase that most closely describes the issue

While tapping the karate point repeat 3 times.

Even though I feel so much fear of the fear I will feel and how I will react to the fear, I deeply and completely love and accept myself.

Even though I feel so much fear of the fear I will feel and how I will react to the fear, I deeply and completely love and accept myself.

Even though I feel so much fear of the fear I will feel and how I will react to the fear, I deeply and completely love and accept myself.

Lightly tapping the eyebrow point about 7 times while saying

I'm so afraid of feeling fear; it's such an uncomfortable feeling

Tap the side of the eye about 7 times while saying

I don't know how I will react to fear, I 'm afraid I will lose control and do something foolish

Tap underneath the eye about 7 times

I'm scared of the feeling of fear during the trade.

Tap under the nose about 7 times

I dread feeling fear during a trade and I'm scared of how I will react

Tap under the mouth above the chin about 7 times

I'm afraid I will be terrified during a trade and freeze up

Tap just under the collar bone about 7 times

I'm terrified I will overreact to the feeling of fear

Tap under the arm pit where it feels a bit sore about 7 times

I hate this out of control feeling I get when I feel fear during a trade

Fear of Letting the Trade Run

This tapping sequence is to deal with fear of letting the trade run and closing trades too early.

Remember you can input your own phrase that most closely describes the issue

While tapping the karate point repeat 3 times.

Even though I feel so much fear when price pulls back against my position during a trade that I close out the trade I deeply and completely love and accept myself.

Even though I feel so much fear when price pulls back against my position during a trade that I close out the trade I deeply and completely love and accept myself.

Even though I feel so much fear when price pulls back against my position during a trade that I close out the trade I deeply and completely love and accept myself.

Lightly tapping the eyebrow point about 7 times while saying
I'm too afraid to let the trade run, I may lose the profits I have made.
Tap the side of the eye about 7 times while saying
I'm frightened when price starts to pull back in case I get stopped out for a loss and lose the money I have made.
Tap underneath the eye about 7 times
I'm scared that if I don't take profits early I will lose the profits I have made.
Tap under the nose about 7 times
I dread feeling that I may lose the profits I have already made.
Tap under the mouth above the chin about 7 times
I'm afraid I will lose the profits I have made and this trade will turn from a winner to a loser.
Tap just under the collar bone about 7 times
I'm terrified I will lose money if I let price pull back on me, it's better to close the trade.
Tap under the arm pit where it feels a bit sore about 7 times
I hate feeling that I will lose my money when price pulls back its better to close the trade than risk losing the profits I have in hand.

EFT UPDATE

When you have mastered the first way of using EFT which is to combine the tapping with a negative statement you can use a more advanced version which is to use the negative statement first followed by a positive statement of what we want. I here is an example.

The EFT Method for Belief in Failure

This tapping sequence is to deal with the belief that we will fail in trading which acts as a filter and causes us to take losing trades and mentally delete the winners

Remember you can input your own phrase that most closely describes the issue
While tapping the karate point repeat 3 times.
Even though I believe I will ultimately fail to be a successful and profitable trader, I really want to be successful in trading.
Even though I believe I will ultimately fail to be a successful and profitable trader, I really want to be successful in trading.
Even though I believe I will ultimately fail to be a successful and profitable trader, I really want to be successful in trading.

Lightly tapping the eyebrow point about 7 times while saying
I know I will fail at trading, I've failed before and I will fail again, however I really want to be successful in trading.
Tap the side of the eye about 7 times while saying
It's too difficult to succeed at trading, that's for other people, smarter people than me, I want to succeed as a trader anyway!

Tap underneath the eye about 7 times
I will fail at trading I don't know why I bother; I really want to be a successful trader.

Tap under the nose about 7 times

I will fail at trading and not be able to provide for myself or my family, even so I want to be successful in my trading career.
Tap under the mouth above the chin about 7 times
I am so scared that I will fail at trading, but I want to be a successful and wealthy trader.

Tap just under the collar bone about 7 times
I am so frightened that after all this work it will be for nothing and I will fail at trading, I want this work to help me be a successful and wealthy trader.

Tap under the arm pit where it feels a bit sore about 7 times
I am a trading failure, In spite of this I want to succeed in trading and be a trading success story.

The EFT Method for Lack of Confidence in Your Trading Analysis

This tapping sequence is to deal with a lack of confidence in our trading analysis and a fear of being wrong.
Remember you can input your own phrase that most closely describes the issue

While tapping the karate point repeat 3 times.

Even though I don't know if I am wrong about this trade I know it still has a lot of value

Even though I don't know if I am wrong about this trade I know it still has a lot of value

Even though I don't know if I am wrong about this trade I know it still has a lot of value

Lightly tapping the eyebrow point about 7 times while saying
I know I am wrong about this trade, I've been wrong before and I will be wrong again, however, I also know this trade will be valuable for my future trading.

Tap the side of the eye about 7 times while saying
I know I'm wrong about this trade and it makes me scared, it's OK to be wrong as long as you learn from it and improve your future performance

Tap underneath the eye about 7 times
I will fail at this trade I don't know why I bother, It's worth the journey, I'm becoming a great trader.

Tap under the nose about 7 times
I'm so scared of being wrong about this trade, however in order to be a great trader I have to be wrong, it's an integral part of my journey, I embrace being wrong about this trade.

Tap under the mouth above the chin about 7 times
I am so scared that I will fail, I want to be right about this trade, however I know that trades that help me learn and become an excellent trader are more valuable.

Tap just under the collar bone about 7 times

I am so frightened that I am wrong about this trade, however I know that being wrong is an essential part of my trading journey and I have to get used to it.

Tap under the arm pit where it feels a bit sore about 7 times
I'm fearful of being wrong about this trade; however I embrace it as a step on my path to future success.

Conclusion

You really don't need to let fear ruin your trading career! If you change your paradigm about losing trades as laid out in the first half of the book , and use the EFT exercises as well as visualisation and affirmations, you will find that your fear should be a thing of the past.

I do offer one-to-one coaching sessions to help if you are having problems implementing the EFT exercises and you can email me if you would like to arrange a session at lrthomasauthor@gmail.com.

You shouldn't need more than one or two sessions to deal with your fear as EFT is so powerful in its effect..

If you have found this book useful please leave me an Amazon review and I will happily send you a PDF copy of this book or another book of your choice for you to print out and make notes. Just email me at lrthomasauthor@gmail.com with the link to the review.

Resources

I hope you have found this book a useful resource in your quest to improve your trading performance. If you have enjoyed this book then please leave me a review on Amazon and as a thank you I will send you a PDF copy of this book or a book of your choice.

I love to hear from my readers so if you have any comments or questions, then you can email me at lrthomasauthor@gmail.com.

Trading Mind-set Video Course
'Create Your trading Success'
Go to www.traderselfcontrol.com to find out more.

Sign up at my blog http://10xroitradingsystem.com/video-courses/ if you would like to learn more about my High ROI Trading Systems.

You can find all my e-books on my Amazon author page or this page on my website.

http://10xroitradingsystem.com/the-ebooks

How to Stop Over-Trading

by

LR Thomas

Trading the financial markets has large potential rewards but also large potential risks.

You must be aware of the risks and be willing to accept them in order to invest in the financial markets. Don't trade with money you can't afford to lose. No representation is made that any account is likely to or will achieve profits or losses similar to any information found in this book. The past performance of any trading system or methodology does not necessarily indicate future results.

Other Books by LR Thomas

Control Your Inner Trader

Overcome Your Fear in Trading

How to Stop Over-trading

The 10XROI Trading System

The Trade Around Your Job System

The High ROI Trading End of Day System

The High ROI Scalping System

Pyramid Your Trades To Profit

How to Learn Forex Without Losing Your Shirt

Table of Contents

How to Stop Over-trading

Over-trading is a generalization for describing one of the most destructive behaviors that a trader can engage in. However the problem with generalizations is that they don't help to pin down the issue to its component parts and analyze where the real problems lie. In order to stop over-trading we need to know what is the specific catalyst that causes us to indulge in that specific over-trading behavior. There may be a few catalysts that mean we over-trade in different ways. When we know specifically what is causing the unwanted behavior we can put in place strategies to stop those specific over-trading behaviors. In this situation knowledge is power.

The Fundamental Reasons for Over Trading

In this book my goal is to help traders understand what is behind over-trading behaviors and more importantly to stop over-trading in its' tracks. That's right, at the end of this book; I hope to cause you to have a paradigm shift in your thinking that will enable you to stop over-trading forever. That's a bold claim and of course I can offer you no guarantees but let me ask you a question?

If you knew a young teenager who was taking Crystal Meth, and you had any influence over that teenager at all, would you know beyond doubt that what they were doing would jeopardize any future happiness and success? Even if the teenager argued that the high they got from Crystal Meth was the best high they had ever felt and that in itself was a good enough reason to continue, would you not do everything you could to explain to that teenager that the current pleasure they felt with the drug could not possibly outweigh the life they would be giving up?

Now if that's the case, imagine that teenager turned around and said to you, this is the best high you will ever feel, why don't you try some and handed you some Meth. In that situation I would hope that you would turn down the drug, even though if you know anything about the effects of Crystal Meth on the brain, you would know that it stimulates the pleasure centers in the brain to a degree that is unmatched by any other drug. You would quite consciously refuse the drug, turning down the instant pleasure in favor of the long term benefits.

This is rather a long question but I hope that as an adult reading this book your answer would be unequivocal, that you would tell the teenager that the short term pleasure of the drug could not possibly outweigh the long term damage that will be done to their health and their life.

So what has this to do with over-trading you may ask? Well when we take trades that are not in the system we can become addicted to the chemical high we get which is the same high that addicted gamblers get when putting on a bet. When we take trades outside our system, we may rationalize it with all sorts of logical reasons, but this is a trick our brains play on us to justify taking a trade and thereby getting a jolt of stimulation which can be similar to the high of taking a drug.

Electronic trading has huge advantages due to its' accessibility however this is also its greatest drawback. There is nothing between you and the mouse when it comes to putting on a trade except your will power and will power has severe limitations. If you have become addicted to the thrill of taking a trade and all that is standing between you and taking a trade that is outside your strategy is your will power, then at some point the addiction will win.

What it comes down to is that we go for the short term intensity of feeling over the long term boring benefit of waiting for the correct setup. I am assuming that readers of this book have experience with the trading environment, if you are new to trading you may not understand how pervasive over-trading is throughout the trading world. However taking trades that are outside the system is probably one of the biggest reasons that traders who have a winning system fail. They simply take trades when they shouldn't and don't take trades when they should. In order to succeed in trading (and this may sound very simplistic) but traders need to take trades when they should and not take trades when they shouldn't. Unfortunately taking trades when they shouldn't can have a knock-on effect which causes traders to miss the trades that are good trades because they get so bruised by their experiences that they avoid trading when it's time to take the trade. They start to mistrust themselves and their system.

The Similarities Between Gambling and Over-trading

There is a common misconception that trading is 'just gambling' but trading to a plan is no more like gambling than professional gambling is like gambling. The difference is fundamental: professional traders and professional gamblers operate to their plan, over-traders and addicted gamblers operate to their emotion.

This doesn't mean that professionals don't feel emotion; it means that they are wary of emotion and put in place strategies that allow them to behave in their own long term best interest.

Here is a very short video showing a table of top class poker players, some of them are laughing and joking and behaving in a very relaxed fashion. The player I want you to look at is top world class poker player Phil Ivey. Notice his attitude, how focused he is, how professional. He is the opposite of a compulsive addicted gambler.

http://tinyurl.com/poker-example

Let's examine the documented effects that gambling has on the human brain, but first of all let me define the difference between

117

gambling and professional gambling as it applies to trading and professional trading.

Gamblers gamble to stimulate certain parts of the brain because it creates an intensity of emotion (dopamine) which stimulates the pleasure centers in the brain. Professional gamblers or Professional traders consciously forgo the pleasures of gambling or trading in favor of the non- stimulating 'waiting for the optimal setup'. When you watch professional poker you will see that the players will throw away most of their hands, only betting on those hands which fit into their calculations as high probability. If they don't it is because they are deliberately trying to throw off the other players as to their playing style so they can't be 'read'. Sometimes you see one of these players go into 'Tilt' a well-known phenomenon in the card playing world. This is where they lose control and start playing hands that have a low probability. This is noticeable because of the heightened emotion displayed by the player, they know they are going into Tilt but they are helpless to do anything about it and they generally end up losing their entire bank roll. Worse than that, they temporarily swapped sides from professional to gambler.

Here is a video showing a professional gambler, famous for being on Tilt. (This gambler generally loses when he plays other top players in his industry; he makes his living trading against less-experienced poker players on-line where he can have easy wins.)

http://tinyurl.com/phil-on-tilt

Here is another video with top poker players talking about what tips them into Tilt.

(Only watch until the first 1 minute 28 seconds)

http://tinyurl.com/top-players-on-tilt

Brain Research That Explains Over-Trading

In an article that appeared in Scientific American they state that the classification for gambling as an addiction has been moved from being classified as a mere compulsion, to a full blown addiction as classified in the DSM, here is an excerpt

In the past, the psychiatric community generally regarded pathological gambling as more of a compulsion than an addiction—a behavior primarily motivated by the need to relieve anxiety rather than a craving for intense pleasure. In the 1980s, while updating the Diagnostic and Statistical Manual of Mental Disorders (DSM), the American Psychiatric Association (APA) officially classified pathological gambling as an impulse-control disorder—a fuzzy label for a group of somewhat related illnesses that, at the time, included kleptomania, pyromania and trichotillomania (hairpulling). In what has come to be regarded as a landmark decision, the association moved pathological gambling to the addictions chapter in the manual's latest edition, the DSM-5, published this past May. The decision, which followed 15 years of deliberation, reflects a new understanding of the biology underlying addiction and has already changed the way psychiatrists help people who cannot stop gambling.

It goes on to say...

The APA based its decision on numerous recent studies in psychology; neuroscience and genetics demonstrating that gambling and drug addiction are far more similar than previously realized. Research in the past two decades has dramatically improved neuroscientists' working model of how the brain changes as an addiction develops. In the middle of our cranium, a series of circuits known as the reward system links various scattered brain regions involved in memory, movement, pleasure and motivation. When we engage in an activity that keeps us alive or helps us pass on our genes, neurons in the reward system squirt out a chemical messenger called dopamine, giving us a little wave of satisfaction and encouraging us to make a habit of enjoying hearty meals and romps in the sack. When stimulated by amphetamine, cocaine or other addictive drugs, the reward system disperses up to 10 times more dopamine than usual.

Continuous use of such drugs robs them of their power to induce euphoria. Addictive substances keep the brain so awash in dopamine that it eventually adapts by producing less of the molecule and becoming less responsive to its effects. As a consequence, addicts build up a tolerance to a drug, needing larger and larger amounts to get high. In severe addiction, people also go through withdrawal—they feel physically ill, cannot sleep and shake uncontrollably—if their brain is deprived of a dopamine-stimulating substance for too long. At the same time, neural pathways connecting the reward circuit to the prefrontal cortex weaken. Resting just above and behind the eyes, the prefrontal cortex helps people tame impulses. In other words, the more an addict uses a drug, the harder it becomes to stop.

OK, so we know that gambling has a similar effect on the brain to drug addiction by stimulating the pleasure centers and giving us a rush of dopamine, however we now also know that as the addiction increases the pleasure decreases. Therefore prolonged gambling addiction does not produce pleasure any more but just stimulates, however the gambler keeps gambling in the hope that they can somehow reproduce the pleasure sensation they first felt when they started out gambling.

Let's get back to over-trading; when we take a trade that is not in our trading system, our brain rationalizes it with a set of good reasons, however the underlying desire is for the brain to stimulate itself by taking action and getting into a trade. So now that you understand this you can take action to bypass the gambling effect on your brain so that when you trade you can use the other part of the brain that professional trader's use which is in the frontal lobe and is associated with delayed gratification and planning.

As a trader starts becoming more skilled they often complain that trading has become boring. That is a clue to what drives their trading and unless traders take action to deal with the boredom they can easily 'crack' and be drawn back into over-trading.

So one explanation for over-trading is that we become addicted to the act of placing trades, which causes us to rationalize to ourselves, just so we can have the sensation of actually clicking the button and feeling those roller coaster emotions.

This is where too much study of trading can have its downside, for example, when you are watching the charts and waiting for a breakout you may well notice that a Gartley pattern or an Elliot wave pattern has set up because of previous learned knowledge. This provides the rationalization your brain is looking for to dive into a trade.

How to Change From a Gambler to a Professional

Whether you are a persistent over-trader or just sometimes lose control, the system to move over from gambling to professionalism is the same. The first step is self-awareness; you need to have that conversation with yourself that you would have had with a teenager taking Crystal Meth. You need to realize that the short term buzz of taking a trade outside your trading plan can be ruinous to your life and your future goals and dreams that involve becoming a successful trader. You then need to make a vow to yourself that you will do everything in your power to stick to your trading plan and never take a trade outside your system ever again!

Do you really want to waste years of your life never getting anywhere in trading because you don't stick to your trading plan? One thing I found helped for me was firstly realizing the seriousness of what I was doing and secondly I took a personal oath.

If you agree that the act of over-trading, which is taking any trade outside your strategy is ruinous to your long term results, then why don't you take a minute now and write down your promise to yourself and sign it, on a piece of paper which you stick to your trading platform or in your diary or anywhere where you will see it on a consistent basis and particularly when you are trading.

Here is what it could say; (write it in your own words to make it meaningful to you)

"I vow never, ever, ever to take a trade that is outside my trading plan ever again. I don't care if price is turning against me, I don't care if I lose this trade, I don't care if I lose every penny in my account in a string of losing trades. I hereby vow that I will stick to my trading plan and never take random trades that fall outside the plan.

I also vow that I will do everything in my power to create a trading routine that includes proper preparation and avoiding fatigue, I will take that routine as seriously as my life because that trading routine is what will enable me to keep that promise to myself.

I further vow that if for any reason I break my oath that I will immediately stop trading and analyze why I entered that trade. I will put into place an amendment to my trading routine to counteract that issue and I will never, ever make that mistake again.

I know if I break this oath and take a trade that is not in my system I am also saying that my life doesn't matter, that my time isn't valuable and I am allowing all the naysayers who think I could never be a successful trader to win. I will not allow that, if I fail at trading I will fail honorably but never because I couldn't stick to my plan!!!!

Signed

(Your Name)

Other Common Causes of Over-trading
Comparing Trading to a Job

A common cause of over- trading is arriving at the charts with the attitude that you are ready for work so now it's time to take trades. In other words, traders subconsciously expect the market to produce trades to their time table rather than subsuming themselves to the market and waiting for the market to produce trades.

This can result in a trader entering a trade prematurely because they haven't done the necessary preparation. The way to cure this is to have a prescribed trading routine which is used prior to the trading day and where the trader sets up their charts, looks at news announcements and does whatever is necessary to create their trading plan for the day.

If a trader comes to the charts and after a couple of hours does not see a trade, they often feel uncomfortable as if they should be doing something. This can cause the trader to enter trades outside their strategy as a way of feeling productive.

People often complain when work goes through quiet periods because they like the buzz of achievement they get from taking action. We are designed to be action takers. Trading is a complete paradigm shift because the essence of trading is non-action.

After years of conditioning that hard work equals achievement it can be a shock to the system to take up an activity like trading where less is most definitely more. In trading you are profitable from the trades you say no to, as well as the trades you say yes to. Trading means sitting on your hands most of the time and this can cause a lot of anxiety because we are not accustomed to it.

This is related to how people are conditioned to view work through school and through a job, which is to turn up and do things. In trading of course it doesn't work like that, most of the time you turn up and do nothing for long periods of time. So how can you get rid of this feeling like you ought to be doing something? Well you can do some other productive things while you are using Forced Checking and waiting for trades to set up. (I will explain Forced Checking later on in this book.)

You could set up a treadmill in front of the screen or a mini gym and spend that time exercising, you could draw or listen to music, what you don't want to do is mental work that will drain your performance when it comes time to take the trade but anything else is fine. A day trader I know spends his time playing video games, but this may not provide the feeling of personal productivity that is provided by doing something more useful.

(One thing I do is to save my ironing until I have to be in front of the charts waiting for an entry which may take up to two hours, I can get a lot of ironing done that way and it keeps my hands off the mouse until it is time to take a trade)

Over-trading Due to No Routine

If you have erratic patterns and come to the charts intermittently with no set routine, you may be so anxious not to miss trades that this can lead to taking trades as they are seen, without the proper analysis. I have done this myself in the past and always found that without the necessary top-down analysis, I was taking a trade that was low probability. The answer is to have a trading routine which is applied whenever you come to your charts and never take a trade without it.

Whatever analysis relates to your particular trading system, whatever steps need to be taken prior to entering a trade this can be written down on a piece of card and stuck to the screen or the desk to remind you not to bypass this process.

Having a regular time to be at the charts helps with this because a process can be developed which starts at a particular time of day and over time that routine turns into a conditioned habit.

Trading Fatigue Due to Diet

The BBC recently aired a Horizon episode which explored the impact of a high-fat, low-carb diet versus a low fat, high carb diet on the cognitive processing of two twin brothers, both doctors. One of the tests involved a spell in an Ameritrade trading room learning to trade stocks with paper money. They were observed by an expert on the affect that diet has on cognitive processing. It became obvious within a very short amount of time that the brother who was on the high fat and protein, low-carb diet was being totally out-classed by the brother on the high-carb low-fat diet. The brother who was on the low fat, high-carb diet had plenty of glucose to fuel the intense level of concentration needed for the different processing tasks the brain was being asked to do. He even commented that he could literally feel his brain working. The brother who was on the low-carb high fat diet by contrast, did not have the glucose to fuel his brain activity and was using ketones, which are a by-product of proteins, which are used for energy when glucose is not available from carbohydrates. This energy was a much inferior source and resulted in much slower processing all round. Going back to the amount of time a human being can maintain concentration, doesn't it make sense that if the brain is being fed inferior fuel, mainly protein and fat, that the quality of the concentration would be less than the person who has the higher carb diet with the superior fuel, glucose from carbohydrates. Most traders are males. Men are statistically less likely to have a high-carb, plant based diet than women.

A 1992 market research study conducted by the Yankelovich research organization concluded that "of the 12.4 million people [in the US] who call themselves vegetarian, 68% are female, while only 32% are male"

Thus if most traders are meat eaters (and by this I include fish, milk, cheese, eggs etc.) and tend towards a high fat diet, their processing is not going to be as good as it could be. This will significantly impact the length of time they are able to maintain quality focus and could easily lead to a loss of will power and a tendency to over-trade.

I have put a snippet of the program on my website here is the link..

http://tinyurl.com/dietandtrading

Ways to Stop Over-Trading

In the previous chapters I have talked about the causes of over-trading firstly as an addiction that produces a chemical reaction in our brain, which makes us rationalize our trades in the brains' attempt to justify the desire for stimulation.

I also talk about the faulty beliefs about trading that traders have, when they compare it to a job in which trading translates to working. Whereas trading in real terms, translates to waiting for the right opportunity. Traders misunderstand on a subconscious level what the real work of trading is which is waiting for the high probability setup.

Traders can also have a faulty belief about the amount of preparation that is needed for a trading day and enter a trade without doing the proper research and find they are taking bad trades because they have no set trading routine.

I also talk about research that shows the quality of our mental processing is strongly affected by our diet, and that a low-fat diet, high in complex carbohydrates, can improve our processing and make traders less susceptible to bad decisions.

In order to help the trader who wants to know how to deal with the problem of over-trading, I am now going to move on from the causes to the cure for over-trading.

Within the term 'over-trading which is a generalization there are specific beliefs and behaviors which result in bad trades. By analyzing exactly where the problems lie, the trader can tackle each problem individually with a preventative strategy which can form an integral part of their trading routine. Let's look at common types of over-trading and some preventative measures that can be put in place.

Doubling Down

I'd like to start with a little story of something I witnessed when I was a new trader and part of a trading room run by a short-term scalper who did not believe in using stops.

When price moved against him he would add to his positions and most of the time price would come back and he would make a profit. However from time to time price would just keep going and he would lose a huge sum which would dwarf all his previous gains.

This is called doubling down and when price is racing away from a trader, he may attempt to alleviate the pain of a certain loss by adding to the losing trade in the hopes that price will turn around. However hope is not a good trading strategy and doubling down is a sure route to decimating a traders' account within a short period of time.

So why do traders double down? Traders double down in order to avoid losses; however the pain of blowing their account usually cures traders of this practice pretty quickly. In my experience doubling down can happen during the cascading effect, when a trader who usually uses stop-losses starts doubling down, it is because they have lost control during the trade and are on Tilt. The way to prevent this is to avoid the cascading effect in the first place, by using strategies that I will cover later in this book.

Recognizing Rationalization

There are all types of rationalizations that a traders' brain makes in order to allow him to take a trade outside his strategy, let me tell you a rationalization I used to make.

'It doesn't matter it's only a practice account'

When I was trading using a demo account and a very small micro account this is the thought that used to pop into my brain directly prior to getting into a trade that I knew I shouldn't take. It happened very fast and the sequence of events went something like this.

Event (usually price moving very fast) Feeling (Wanting to get into the trade , fear of missing out) Thought (I must stick to my system , this isn't in my trading plan) Rationalization (It's OK it's only a small practice account just take the trade to see what happens.)

Let me give you another rationalization process not connected to trading.

Walking around the supermarket (hungry) and hitting the chocolate aisle.

Event (seeing my favorite dark chocolate with chili), Feeling(I want that chocolate) Thought,(this is not in my eating plan, I didn't want it until I saw it today), Rationalization (I'll have it today, I can always just have a little taste and save the rest for another time, in any case I'll start my diet tomorrow.) You can see the brain tricks us by giving us good reasons to justify taking the action that will give us short term pleasure over the long term pleasure of being healthy or waiting for the correct set-up and avoiding bad trades.

The Role of Time in Rationalization

Tomorrow is a huge factor in rationalization; the trader /dieter says to themselves that today they can do the thing that they know they shouldn't because they can do the thing that they know they should, tomorrow.

So how does one deal with rationalization? The answer is to outsmart your brain. So how can you outsmart your brain? The answer is in preparation and awareness. Let's go back to the trip around the supermarket, firstly, I make sure that I am not hungry when I go round, secondly, I make sure that I have a list that I keep referring to, thirdly, I make sure that I don't go down the sweet aisle and fourthly, if a rationalization does pop into my head that reasons that it is OK to buy that Chili Chocolate then I recognize it for what it is, my brain making up excuses to get me to take action against my best interests.

So how can rationalizations be overcome in trading? Let me give you an example, let's say you make careful notes of what situations cause you to lose control and take trades outside of your trading plan. You find that one situation is that when you are watching the charts you see another trade set up that is related to another system you have learned in the past. You also find that if this situation happens after an hour of watching the charts you have a very strong impulse to enter that trade. Now this is a scenario that is very likely to happen, most experienced traders have made their way through a good number of trading systems and there is the residue of all those systems in their memory which can easily spill over into their chart analysis. So what type of strategies could deal with this urge to enter a setup outside a trading plan? Well you could add to the trading plan that if you see any other setup besides the one you are waiting for, you will ignore it. You could also create a small card which is stuck to the corner of the screen saying 'Ignore everything except the plan'

Word it positively rather than negatively for example say 'Stick to the plan' rather than 'Don't trade outside the plan' Another strategy is to take frequent breaks, take a five minute break every half hour, this would refresh your brain and relieve the tension of waiting for a set-up, lessening the temptation of taking an unplanned trade.

The next stage is to test the strategy and measure the results, keep tweaking until the problem of taking trades that are related to past trading systems is completely resolved.

Avoid Temptation

If you avoid those events which will cause you to rationalize an entry you greatly reduce the chance of taking trades outside your strategy. However if your trading system is designed in such a way that it exposes you to temptation then you are much more likely to crack and start over-trading.

Common Triggers to Over-trading

Here are the common triggers that cause over-trading, together with strategies to defeat them. You can use the same process to deal with your own personal over-trading triggers.

Loss of Will Power During Day Trading

If you are a day trader and spend a lot of time in front of the charts you are far more likely to lose control. When you lose control this can lead to a cascading effect which is that a small loss of control can open the floodgates to all sorts of other negative trading behaviors. In our example we will use a mythical day trader, Jack.

Jack is waiting for a setup and watching the 15 minute charts, he is waiting for a change of direction in the market and then his plan is to wait for a pull-back to the breakout area together with a confirming candle pattern, to be formed prior to entry so he has a defined place to place a small stop loss. After 2 hours have passed, price has formed a sideways pattern on the 15 minute chart but has not yet broken out, however by this time Jacks' will-power that has prevented him jumping into an impulsive trade has been eroded; he is mentally tired and very vulnerable to taking trades outside his strategy. Price starts to break out of the sideways move and Jack takes the trade, even though the trade has not been confirmed by Jacks' criteria for entry. Because of the loss of control the breakout has formed the basis of the rationalization to trade outside the plan. Price then drops down back inside the breakout zone and Jack is now in a losing position. He rationalizes that price will break back out again in his direction and moves the stop loss further away to 'allow the trade room to breathe', another rationalization

Price then breaks out the other side of the breakout zone and runs in the opposite direction. Jack is now holding a large loss with no hope of price reversing in his direction. (This is a classic situation where a trader starts doubling down in the hopes that price will turn around and move them back to break even.) Jack now has most of his account at risk, and at this point he is praying. Glory of glories, price does move back and reaches a point where Jack is at breakeven. Now another part of Jacks' brain, the part that wants to be justified in this behavior, whispers in his ear, "maybe I can turn this trade into a big win" and instead of closing out the trade Jack lets it run. Only now it turns round and starts moving against him very fast, the previous return was just a pullback in an overall change of direction. Jack now stands there watching helplessly as his account is decimated. Eventually he closes the trade. He has just lost 50% of his account. Now, he is shaking and without thinking he dives back into the market, he now has to win it all back. If Jack is lucky he will quit before he loses his whole account.

The problem here is that the structure of Jacks' trading system was psychologically flawed, it may have back tested as a profitable system, however it did not back test as a psychologically sound system. The long hours at the charts left him vulnerable to tiredness and loss of will power which caused a small slip, which then led to a whole cascade of destructive trading behaviors. Here is how Jack could redesign his system so this does not happen.

Step One – Forced Checking

While he is waiting for price to change direction he uses a technique called 'Forced Checking'. This is where he checks the computer every 30 -60 minutes to see if price has changed direction. (He times the checking so he doesn't miss it if it should set up while he is away from the charts. The check takes no more than 10 seconds; he closes the platform and GOES AWAY AND DOES SOMETHING ELSE. This something else could be anything that takes Jack away from his trading platform but that doesn't drain his mental energy and can be picked up and put down at a moments' notice.

Step Two –Price Alerts

Price then forms a sideways channel, Jack has spotted this in good time and sets text alerts so that he knows when price breaks out of the sideways channel and then he closes the charts and GOES AND DOES SOMETHING ELSE.

Step Three – Back to Forced Checking

Price then breaks out of the sideways channel, if, as in our example it breaks in the wrong direction then Jack has been protected from over-trading and blowing his account. However in this example the trade goes in Jacks' direction and price has broken out of the channel. Jack then uses forced checking to wait for the confirmation pull-back to the break-out area and the confirming area of support/resistance.

Step Four –The Entry

Finally the entry candle pattern sets up, six hours after Jack first started waiting for the entry. However by using these two strategies, he is mentally fresh and takes the entry, puts in his stop loss and take profit and then closes the platform. He also uses forced checking to monitor his trade which keeps him from interfering with the trade and going against his take profit plan.

These two strategies, Forced Checking and Text Alerts, when added to the Jack's system, allow him to spend minimum time at the charts so he doesn't have to use his will-power. Every time he opens his platform he knows what he is looking for, and if the trade isn't yet ready he closes the platform and goes back to his other activity. This is similar to what happens when baking a cake, you check the oven to see if the cake is ready and if it isn't ready you simply close the oven and go back to doing something else.

Trading During Specific Times

Another way to protect a day traders' emotional state is to trade during specific times. For example there is a day trading strategy known as 'The London Close System (there is a link in the resource section of the book for highly recommended third party tools, if interested). This trading system as its' name suggests takes place during a very specific time period the end of the London trading session. This means that the trader is only waiting for an entry from about 3.30 to 5.30 GMT time. A period of a maximum of two hours,

133

what is more Forced Checking can also be used during this time period so a trader does not have to spend these two hours glued to the charts and getting mentally tired. He can use checking to wait for the trigger event. During the trade the trader has to be at the screen actively monitoring the trade and by using Forced Checking prior to the entry they have saved up their mental energy for when they need it.

Indicators That Can Help to Stop Over-trading

There are some Metatrader alert indicators that can help when the trading system does not use horizontal support resistance.

Fibonnaci Alert Indicators

These indicators can provide an automated text alert when price hits a particular Fibonacci level.

Trend Lines

These indicators can provide an automated text alert when price hits a trend line, or breaks through a trend line.

Price Patterns and Candle Patterns

Autochartist pattern recognition software is provided free if you have a live account with most brokers, and spots chart patterns on most time frames.

There are also MT4 Indicators which can provide text alerts when a price pattern or a candle pattern is spotted.

I don't trade stocks so I don't know the software stock traders use, however I am sure stock traders can find similar alert software by searching on Google.

Flawed Day Trading Systems

Any manual day trading system which cannot be adapted to using Forced Checking and alert indicators is fundamentally flawed. The reason is that built into the system is the probability that the trader will lose their self-control, due to tiredness and is much more likely to over-trade. The solution is to find a system which is designed in such a way so you can use these strategies to protect your mental energy.

If your trading system is not designed for forced checking, but is profitable then you can use structured breaks, be aware that sometimes this could result in missed trades but overall the benefits more than make up for any lost trades.

This applies even if you are using very short term time frames such as the one minute charts. If you are using the 1 minute charts you could take a 5 minute break every 30 minutes. This means becoming very sensitive to your own physical well-being and not getting completely caught up in the charts. You leave the charts well before you start getting tired and have a break. You will trade better on your return than if you had just spent the entire time watching the charts. To highlight the value of regular breaks here is an article that appeared in the New York Times.

In the 1950s, the researchers William Dement and Nathaniel Kleitman discovered that we sleep in cycles of roughly 90 minutes, moving from light to deep sleep and back out again. They named this pattern the Basic-Rest Activity Cycle or BRAC. A decade later, Professor Kleitman discovered that this cycle recapitulates itself during our waking lives.

The difference is that during the day we move from a state of alertness progressively into physiological fatigue approximately every 90 minutes. Our bodies regularly tell us to take a break, but we often override these signals and instead stoke ourselves up with caffeine, sugar and our own emergency reserves — the stress hormones adrenaline, noradrenaline and cortisol.

Working in 90-minute intervals turns out to be a prescription for maximizing productivity. Professor K. Anders Ericsson and his colleagues at Florida State University have studied elite performers, including musicians, athletes, actors and chess players. In each of these fields, Dr. Ericsson found that the best performers typically practice in uninterrupted sessions that last no more than 90 minutes. They begin in the morning, take a break between sessions, and rarely work for more than four and a half hours in any given day.

"To maximize gains from long-term practice," Dr. Ericsson concluded, "individuals must avoid exhaustion and must limit practice to an amount from which they can completely recover on a daily or weekly basis."

So, if the best performers in the world structure rest breaks into their daily practice, then trading, which puts a huge cognitive strain on traders is no different. The way to do it is to be alert when it is time to be alert and relaxed during the rest of the time. This is very different from how most day traders are, which is, they attempt to stay alert from the time they are at the charts, all the way until lunch-time, or when they finish trading for the day.

What is the difference between my day trading system and the average day trading system?

For this example I am going to use my High ROI Scalping System which is a day-trading system so I can compare like with like. The average day-trading system requires you to watch the charts continuously waiting for an event to occur. When you watch the charts continuously, you will be exposed to temptation to enter trades that are outside your strategy.

In my High ROI Scalping System I use a system where I check the charts once an hour, and then ONLY if I know there is a potential setup; if there is no setup approaching I don't check the charts. This results in a huge reduction in actual screen time.

When I am waiting for a break of a horizontal level I put in a price alert on my mobile phone, which I carry around with me, so I can get straight back to the charts and take the entry if it is a confirmed set-up. I don't have to watch the charts continuously for more than 30 minutes at any one time, which is the time of entry, and it is normally less than that.

When I do check the charts, I look at the charts for a minute at the most to see if price has reached the hourly trend line. If price does reach the level I am waiting for, at that point I will switch to a five minute chart. I then use two different strategies, Forced Checking every fifteen minutes and Distraction.

The distraction is that I have a separate screen where I watch a TV program while doing something with my hands which could be sorting socks or ironing. This keeps my brain and hands busy while I am still watching the five minute charts and dilutes the tension of waiting for an entry.

I have designed these strategies into my trading routine to make sure that I am not exposed to temptation by random events, because my chart watching is only confined to those minutes when I am actually supposed to enter a trade. During that time when I am waiting for an entry I use the strategy of distraction in order to reduce the tension of waiting. I deliberately designed the system in that way because I have Attention Deficit Disorder which makes me more than usually prone to lack of impulse control.

When you have ADD you have to outsmart your brain in order to get things done, so a high degree of self-knowledge is a requisite part of

137

self-help. What I am suggesting is that you look at over-trading in the same way, which is that your brain is wired to over-trade and that putting in place safeguards within your system which prevent you sabotaging yourself, are an essential part of maintaining your discipline.

The Problem with Relying on Willpower and Self-Discipline

Do self- disciplined people really have more will-power than the rest of us or do they naturally develop techniques that enable them to avoid temptation?

In a now famous psychology experiment a Canadian professor Walter Mischel carried out what is known as The Marshmallow Test. He gathered a group of four year olds in a room with a bowl of marshmallows. He told them that they could either have one marshmallow now, or they could have two if they waited until the researcher came back into the room. The results were that most of the children couldn't wait and opted for the single marshmallow, however some of the children were able to wait until the researcher came back into the room twenty minutes later. This experiment is often cited because when the researchers followed up with the children years later, when they were adults, those who were able to delay gratification were overall far more successful in life than the other children. However did those children really have more will power and discipline than those other children? or did they employ strategies which enabled them to wait. When the behavior of the children who resisted the marshmallows was analyzed, it was found that they used distraction techniques, such as singing and pulling their hair to distract them from the sweets. See a video of the re-created experiment at the link below.

http://tinyurl.com/marshmallow-test-video

In another experiment Mischel told the children that they should imagine that the marshmallows were fluffy clouds instead of marshmallows, and using this thinking strategy also enabled the children to last much longer before succumbing to the temptation of the sweets.

The problem with will power and self-discipline is that they are finite resources. In trading, if you rely on your will power and self-discipline to avoid the temptation of getting into a trade outside your strategy, you are setting yourself up for failure. The answer is to put in place strategies that make it much easier to avoid temptation. The less discipline and will power you are required to exert, the more likely you are to succeed with your trading system

Here is an excerpt from a Stanford journal on will-power.

One of the most replicated findings in the field of willpower research is that people who use willpower seem to run out of it. Interestingly, any act of self-control leaves people with less willpower for completely unrelated challenges. Trying to control your temper, ignore distractions or refuse seconds all tap the same source of strength. The research also shows that willpower decreases over the course of the day, as your energy gets "spent" on stress and self-control. This has become known as "the muscle model" of willpower. Like your biceps or quadriceps the willpower "muscle" can get exhausted from effort.

It goes on to say

Two things have been shown to train the brain's willpower reserve, or strength: meditation and physical exercise.

Meditation training improves a wide range of willpower skills, including attention, focus, stress management, impulse control and self-awareness. It changes both the function and structure of the

brain to support self-control. For example, regular meditators have more gray matter in the prefrontal cortex. And it doesn't take a lifetime of practice — brain changes have been observed after eight weeks of brief daily meditation training.

Physical exercise also leads to similar changes in the brain, especially the pre-frontal cortex; however it's not clear why. Regular exercise – both intense cardiovascular training and mindful exercise like yoga — also makes the body and brain more resilient to stress, which is a great boost to willpower

The other solution as mentioned in the research is to build up your will-power by using techniques such as meditation, exercise and constant practice. These techniques can be combined with the techniques I suggest to create optimum effectiveness. However these tactics also require self-discipline and so I prefer the simple way, which is to avoid having to use will-power as much as possible.

Over-trading as a Response to Stress

A very common reason that traders over-trade is that they have a hard time with their trading. For example, they have had a series of losses, or they get stopped out and see price racing away from them in the right direction. It may also be stress that is due to events that are going on outside trading. This build-up of stress is released by taking a trade.

This can set a dangerous precedent, if every time there is a build-up of stress it is released by trading when you shouldn't and this habit gets hard wired into your neurology, it will be very difficult to succeed as a trader.

However this behavior can be changed. There are two ways to approach this, one way is to be aware of what is happening and make sure that you leave the charts before things get to a state that you are likely to trade badly. For example, let's say you have had a bad day and are feeling depressed and anxious. The best way to ensure that you are in the right mind-set to trade is to do a pre-trade check list which includes a mood meter, which becomes part of your trading routine. If your emotional level is not right then you have two choices you can either walk away or you can do something to change your emotional state.

Most traders won't do this, however after you have blown your account a number of times simply because you traded when you were feeling bad, this provides a strong motivation to take a check of how you feel. Now what you can then do is use EFT, meditation, self-talk, music yoga or anything that can change your mood before you trade.

(EFT stands for Emotional Freedom Technique which I cover extensively in my other books, Control Your Inner trader and Overcome Your Fear in Trading.) If the emotional upset is due to an event outside trading then you can use calming strategies to make sure you deal with it before heading to the charts.

You see when you are a trader you have to practice extreme self-love. You have to look after yourself as if you were your own child. That means looking after your emotional and physical well-being. You need to take care of yourself emotionally because you are the variable in your trading system. You need to make sure that you are in tiptop working order in order to trade well.

Over-trading After a String of Losses

Every trading system will go through losses and if you are trading your system well, then the losses will be a normal part of trading your system. However the problem that traders have is that they never really know for sure whether this string of losses is due to their system not being viable anymore in the market.

However well a system has performed in the past, you can never know for sure if it will perform the same way in the future. If you did know this for sure it would be much easier to handle a string of losses. Equally, even if you know that the system in the past has had a maximum losing streak of five losses in a row, you never know if this is the time that you will have a losing streak of fifty-five losses in a row and this is the time you wipe out your account!

It is this uncertainty and thinking process that lies behind the feeling of despair that can overtake a trader who is going through a losing streak and the trader needs a mental paradigm as well as a practical solution to protect both their trading account and their mental health.

You need to have a method of determining if the losses are the normal system losses or if you are doing something different in your trading. How can you determine this? Well if you keep extensive records of every trade which include the emotional state you were in when you took the trade then you should be able to spot if you are trading badly. The danger of being in a slump that is due to you trading badly is that you can trade your capital away so you must know the difference!

Traders avoid keeping records so they don't have to face what is really going on when they trade but when you are committed to becoming the best trader you can be then keeping extremely detailed notes is in integral part not only of improving your trading but also being able to spot when something is off. You get to know yourself better by looking at how you behaved under stress and can put in place strategies to help you deal better with the pressures of trading.

Here are some practical techniques which could be adopted to deal with losing streaks. Use a few different trading systems which can be easily traded in tandem. Thus if one system stops working as it should, it will only affect a small part of your overall account. You could put in place a rule which says if a system starts to perform differently than it has in the past, for example if the maximum string of losses was five and it now has a losing streak of ten, then you put the system on pause until you determine whether the system now has a different set of parameters or is simply not working anymore. Another practical solution is to have separate accounts using different money management techniques. These strategies can help protect the trader emotionally as well as save their account. They now have a strategy in place to help them deal with the failure of the trading system.

How to Think About Trading - A New Paradigm

Many traders make the fundamental mistake of attributing their problems in trading to their own weakness. Let's get this straight; trading is an activity that is uniquely designed to be difficult for the human psychology. Most traders have the same types of problems, why is that? It is because the human brain is not designed to be a good trader.

There is a relatively new branch of economics called Behavioral Economics championed by the well-known author Daniel Kahneman, author of Thinking Fast and Slow. Traditional economics operates on the assumption that people will invariably act in their own best interest, however this is so often not the case that Behavioral Economics was developed as a way to scientifically explain the many times people don't act in their own best interest particularly when making financial decisions.

Trading is behavioral economics in play; traders are hard wired to make the wrong decisions when trading. They act against their own best interest and this is across the board. The traders that win have found a way to outsmart their own brain and that includes a way to think about trading.

I have a video on my blog which shows Daniel Kahneman talking about the problems of trading at this link.

http://10xroitradingsystem.com/inner-trader-tips/

So how can changing the way you think about trading in general help you become a better trader and stop over-trading? Most traders get into trading as a way to make money, that means that all the decisions that are made relating to their trades are to do with making money and are therefore subject to the flaws of behavioral economics.

Supposing there was a different way of thinking about trading which is not only to make money but to become a better person who is able to overcome challenges! If you look at your trading as a way to increase your mental stamina and fortitude then when a difficult situation comes up, such as a string of losses, your focus is now on your behavior and your source of achievement is in the fact that you stuck to prepared strategy for dealing with losses and did not use this as an excuse to over-trade.

In the British television show of 'I'm a celebrity get me out of here', you get a bunch of celebrities thrown together in the middle of the jungle who undergo grueling experiences on prime time TV. Now of course these celebrities go on TV in order to raise their profile but what also happens is that we get an intimate look at those people who really thrive in that situation and eagerly accept each new challenge and those who are whittled out very early on. The difference is that some of the celebrities look on this experience as a challenge which will help them to grow and each challenge that enables them to grow as a person is approached with a sense of adventure to see how they will perform under extreme pressure.

Another phenomenon is the rise of charity sponsored events in far-flung places involving hard physical activity such as a bike ride across the desert. These types of activities have massively increased in popularity. It is not only to raise money for charity, the people who are doing the event are signing up for an experience they know will be extremely difficult and challenging and they do it in order to meet challenges head on and grow as a person. This attitude helps them to face hard physical conditions and mental challenges which are part and parcel of the experience. In its own way the act of trading provides some of the hardest mental training conditions out there. If human beings are intrinsically wired to be bad traders and the only way to overcome these challenges is to undergo extreme mental hardship in order to forge a new way of being around your trading platform, then it makes sense that a similar attitude to trading to the people who cycle across the desert may help.

Supposing trading was seen not just as an opportunity to get rich but as an opportunity to grow as a human being? In the same way that people train for the marathon or climb mountains, traders would be prepared for mental hardship and that's the point, it's what a trader has overcome and conquered that makes the trading experience so rich.

So how could this apply to over-trading, well taking trades that are outside your strategy is a response to some kind of stress, it may be the stress of a previous losing streak, or an outside event or a response to watching the charts for too long and getting tired. If you were going to climb a mountain you would be prepared for the hardships ahead, you would mentally prepare and analyze each stage of the climb and make sure you had the necessary equipment and strategies. What I am suggesting is that you prepare for those events that would normally lead you to over-trade both practically and emotionally, by practicing new responses and having a new mental paradigm which sees trading as the ultimate mental challenge.

Now the reason most traders do not adopt this mind-set right from the beginning of their trading career is that trading looks like a deceptively easy endeavor compared to bike riding across the desert. Traders get into trading to make easy money not to become great, and develop themselves as a trader or as a person. If they wanted to do that they would be reading Tony Robbins and Brian Tracy not taking up trading. However that is what trading truly is and it is not spelled out in any trading courses you buy, you have to find it out the hard way. Trading is a test of your mental and emotional courage and fortitude unlike many other mental type activities. Nothing really prepares you for trading and the stress it places on a trader. Many traders have committed suicide, think of Jesse Livermore, one of the greatest traders of all time, who committed suicide after he lost his third fortune.

This shows how essential it is to take care of your trading psychology right from the beginning of your trading journey so you don't succumb to stress and depression and over-trade as a response.

Psychological Danger Spot System Mapping

The way I advise to mentally prepare for each trading danger spot is to review your trading system in a new way. I call it Psychological Danger Spot System Mapping. What you do is examine each part of your system for those areas which induce psychological stress; you also keep rigorous notes on your emotional state and what is going in your life when you take a trade. When you do this you will be able to see your response to each trading challenge as if you were an outsider looking on. You can then put in place strategies to prevent yourself getting into the sort of situations that would cause you to over-trade and to deal with the inevitable emotions that arise.

Determining System Danger Points

Any part of your system which relies on you exerting will power is a danger spot. Let's look at potential danger spots in a typical day trading system.

Danger Spot One

Watching the charts for long periods while waiting for an entry. Any system that requires you to stay in front of the charts for long periods of time waiting for an entry is testing your will power and is just asking for trouble. You may start out strong willed but after an hour or so your resistance wears down and the longer you have to wait the more likely it is that you will succumb to the temptation to break the tension of waiting by entering a trade that is outside your system.

Solution

Ideally your trading system does not require you to stay in front of the charts for long periods of time, (if you are interested in High ROI trading systems that require very little screen time, then check out the resources section at the end of the book).

However if it does, and that causes you to over-trade, then a solution is to take frequent breaks, even if the risk is that you miss a trade. Also take a short break after you have closed out a trade. Go for a short walk around the block, or sit in the garden or anything that takes your mind off the charts and allows your brain to rest. Time the breaks so that you are taking at least one break per hour and ideally two. This is essential if you are a day-trader or scalper who has to spend long hours in front of the charts. Ideally you want to end the day still mentally fresh.

Danger Spot Two

You have a series of losses and you lose control and start to take trades with a 'don't care' attitude. This leads to taking risky trades in an attempt to win back your profits

147

Solution

There is no one size fits all solution there is only a solution that works for you. One of my students does some scalping and limits his trades to three if he has a series of either three wins or three losses. This is built into his system and is designed to prevent losing control and over-trading.

Designing a system in such a way that it protects you from your own weaknesses is a really smart idea.

Danger Spot Three

Coming to the charts and trading without a plan. Many newbie traders start off without taking their trading seriously and come to the charts without doing the necessary pre-trade analysis, unfortunately this is asking for impulsive trading behaviors.

Solution

Create a trading routine which includes all pre-trade analysis and mentally prepares you for the trading day. Have a trading plan , which is an outline of an event that you are waiting for in order to look for a trade and then an entry. For example you may be looking for a particular price level; well there is no need to even look at the charts until you have received a text alert that the level has been hit. If you have planned out what you are waiting for before you go in front of the charts then you are far less likely to succumb to temptation when price gyrates up and down.

Think of how a cat reacts when you dangle a piece of string in front of him, you don't want to be like a cat chasing every movement that passes before their eyes, you want to be like the cheetah stalking their prey and waiting perhaps for days for a sign of weakness that signals an easy kill.

By keeping extensive records you will soon be able to spot the psychological danger spots in your own system and come up with strategies to overcome these. I have also provided some exercises that can help deal with over-trading issues in my other books, Control Your Inner Trader and Overcome Your Fear in Trading. (See the resource section at the end of the book for details.)

Comments From Students About Over-trading

Here are some comments from my students about over trading that you may find helpful. I have kept their identities confidential so I am just using their initials.

AJ

Overtrading and me!

A lot of people who I know, start trading for one of the reasons to become financially independent and get out of the job that they hate, trade from home, have and independent lifestyle. The second is to overcome debt. I started trading for both of these reasons.

There is no harm in having both of these motivations to trade, but the issue comes with how quickly you want to achieve both of these. I was 24 when I started trading, being hot blooded there were only two ways I could achieve my freedom from both my job and my student loan. One was placing big trades and the other, keep looking at the screen all possible times, to avoid the missed chance of a trade. In hindsight both were risky behaviors.

I got into this habit of wrecking my accounts, every time I believed that I was on the verge of making it big, I used a new strategy, a new EA, applying 5-7 strategies in one account and when one starts spending so much time looking at the screens one lives in the fear of having to make money and forcing trades even when there were no opportunities.

What finally happened was I ran a huge debt on six credit cards, it became so bad that I had to borrow money from money lenders at 5% per month (yes per month) to pay my debts. I had to stop trading; I had money lenders calling me all the time. I was forced to give up trading. It would be another three years before I would trade again and trade well, not big money but not very bad either.

I would like to highlight some things that changed from then and now

I sorted out issues of trading – basically debts, and money for living, saved a little. I don't have to think of my next meal coming from Forex, or my next mortgage payment.

Since what made it worse in the first place was looking at the charts all the time, changing already placed orders, taking trades when no opportunity really existed, this time around keeping busy with work forces discipline

I no more look at the charts from a 5, 15 minute perspective but rather a Daily, 4hr and 1 hr chart.

I now spend less than 1 hour over the weekend and less than 20 minutes on weekdays looking for trade setups.

I also realize that there is no point of sitting and looking at the charts all day, in the forex world, you don't have to worry about missed opportunities, there will be a new one tomorrow

Strategies like the 10XROI, and Pyramid your trades, improves your probability many times over.

(Aside: These are my trading systems you can find the links in the resource section at the end of the book)

LB

Revenge trading is a common trigger for over trading. This is especially true immediately after a loss where you just have to get back into the market as soon as possible to get "your" money back.

This is only human nature to feel "emotional pain" after a trading loss and an overwhelming desire to take high risk trades to just get "your" money back. The trading plan (if there is one!) is put to one side "for the moment". Trades are often entered without any real setup just a feeling that you are sure the market will turn in your favor soon. The result is over trading especially if the next trade is also a loser!

The solution, of course, is to have discipline to follow your plan, but sometimes that is very much easier said than done!

So what do we do?

Here are some practical actions to take after experiencing a trading loss.

Shut down the trading platform and/or charting package and ...

(1) Go for a short walk to clear your head. I often walk to the local shop and buy a newspaper and find that just 10 or 15 minutes away from the computer is sufficient to overcome the urge to revenge trade.

(2) Do some exercises such as Yoga or Pilates, or maybe lift a few weights etc.

(3) Spend some time meditating. If you haven't done this before the following book is excellent and comes with a useful CD.

"Mindfulness: A practical guide to finding peace in a frantic world" by Mark Williams & Danny Penman

(4) Or you can fill in your own action here
_____ ... But remember it only needs to
be 10 or 15 minutes to be effective.

AF

I have built some specific rules into my trading plan for dealing with
that issue.

So now if my first two - three trades of the day are winners (if I am
scalping, rather than swing/position trading), I stop trading before
euphoria and feelings of omnipotence take over the trash-bin that is
my mind and I go back to square one on a serious loser.

I do something similar now if the first two - three trades of the day are
losers so that I am not tempted to revenge trade (to make up for the
losses) - a recipe for further and compounding losses.

Also keeping a trading journal for each trade - and recording one's
emotional frame of mind for either a win or a loss helps - as I can see
the warning signals or patterns more easily.

Really, your High ROI approach for swing/position trading is an ideal
way to let the trade come to me - and if I follow your setup rules,
over-trading is no longer an issue for me. (aside: See these trading
systems in resource section at the end of the book)

RA

I have never really over traded. The only time I have been tempted to,
is when I have set a points target for a week.

Comment: Setting a target puts a trader under pressure to create a
result that is ultimately not in their control, suppose they feel bad that

week, or there are no trades to take? I advise my students to use Process Thinking rather than Results Thinking which prevents this type of scenario.

SB

As a new trader, over trading is something that I have fallen foul of and luckily I have realized quite quickly the detrimental impact this can have on your trading account. I think one of the main problems is that in most things in life, it is accepted that the harder you work, the more you can expect to be compensated, be it monetarily or by any other means of satisfaction. It has become apparent to me that this ingrained work ethic or ethos does not transfer well to the trading environment. I strongly believe you do have to work hard to become a successful trader however this does not mean you have to constantly trade. I have found that personally, a way to overcome this problem has been to submerse myself in learning about all aspects of trading and putting my effort into reading about trading psychology, market behavior and spending a lot of time writing and re-writing trading plans, setting myself objectives and getting a clear picture in my head of where I want to be in the future. Spending all this time doing these tasks has meant that I cannot possibly sit and look at live charts all the time.

I think when people first start trading, there is definitely an excitement to be had by putting on a trade regardless of the outcome, this is where trading has a strong correlation with gambling. Judging by most of the trading systems out there, people seem to be attracted to scalping and I feel this is the easiest way to get bogged down by over-trading. It is only natural that if you are sitting staring at a screen for hours on end, you will take trades that do not meet your criteria, simply because you want to feel the buzz of putting on that trade.

You justify to yourself the reasons why you have taken it and then you slowly watch the trade turn against you and the next thing you do is start to become emotional about this little loss and you take another trade based on anger and frustration. Before you know it, you have lost a lot of capital and then you realize you have just wasted a whole day losing money. The sooner you can realize what is happening the better. I felt myself falling into this trap and so I decided only to use the longer term charts for my underlying analysis and only then move down to a smaller time frame to get a better entry. Therefore I am not sitting watching charts all day, only when the daily, weekly, monthly charts have indicated that it might be prudent to do so.

I actually think that over-trading is probably a much bigger problem than many people realise, experienced traders included. II think that if you over-trade, all the other negative trading behaviours (fear, greed, revenge trading, impatience, letting losses get out of hand, cutting profits short etc.) will surface sooner or later and a kind of snowball effect will occur.

When it comes to trading, I really think that less is definitely more, and the sooner that a trader can realize this then the better off they will be. That being said, if you have a methodology and a system that you believe in, take the trades that meet your criteria without hesitation and with the knowledge that any individual trade has an uncertain future but your belief in your edge mean that the probabilities are in your favor in the long run.

CF

One issue that I have faced is setting and following the rule that says after X losses or loss of X5, STOP trading!

FXoutlier

I think that over-trading is caused by one thing, stress. Ok, it happens during euphoria as well, but euphoria usually comes after a period of stress. Once it manifests itself, it can become a bad habit unless somehow kept in check. Once it becomes a habit, then we all know how difficult habits are to change.

It is the same as over-eating. Many people over-eat, or eat unhealthily, when under periods of stress. When the period of stress ends, they celebrate by eating more. When they come out of it after the celebrations wear off, they decide enough is enough and take action to lose weight and live healthily until the next period of stress occurs.

It's almost as if something is switched off in the brain, so we lessen our guard and take risks with our health or our trades, or our credit card debt or gambling at cards etc. when we are under stress. We become desperate.

With trading we often start off relaxed enough, but a poor run, not finding any trades, not being able to break out of breaking even, can set it off. One more loser can be the tipping point, when we lose our discipline or even a winner that you eventually get. Get two winners and you think you've made the break through and your guard then can be really down.

We also get stressed when there is too much info, indicators etc. on our charts and we don't really understand what it is we're trying to do. No well-defined simple plan.

Losers stress us because we've never sat down through a forwards testing period that has given us a large enough sample of results to say that, yes, it is possible, but I'm likely to get losing periods of 5, 6 , 7 or 8 or more and I have to ignore them or scale down size during the period and work our way out. When starting out, these losing runs will be even bigger, as we aren't selective enough, all adding to the stress. Not enough time spent learning our craft with small stakes, because we all want to dive in and make money. Losing money, that is stressful. Compound that with the lack of a plan, no testing results, no understanding ourselves, then bang the button is switched off and we over trade.

There are similarities with the panic button that people without enough experience get in certain high risk situations. Suddenly people freeze and everything is a blur. The fog of war sets in. Something switches off, the world outside seems to slow down. Malcolm Gladwell's Blink and David and Goliath give examples of this. This can be overcome by practice, training, drilling, exercises, so we are confident in what we are to do in a certain situation, like our testing period in trading. We are confident that we know what to do because we have a plan and rules that we have practiced over and over, so we aren't put under as much stress, and we deal with the unplanned stuff more easily.

Over-trading and Lack of Accountability

In banks the traders have a risk manager, someone who oversees their trades and keeps an eye on the trader to make sure they are not taking on too much risk. Horror stories of traders like Nick Leeson who brought down Barings Bank force banks to make sure that risk is tightly scrutinized. The problem is that a day-trader sitting at home has no level of accountability. This is where an accountability buddy can help. If you can find a fellow day-trader, someone you can chat to during the day, someone who will hold you accountable for taking stupid trades then you are much less likely to take a trade outside the system parameters.

However what can you do if you don't have a trading buddy and you are day-trading? How can you keep your self-control so that after a series of losses or other events outside your control you don't start revenge trading and taking trades outside your system parameters?

This goes to the heart of something I talk about a lot in my other book, Control Your Inner Trader and Overcome Your Fear in Trading. It involves making your goals process goals rather than results goals. When a trader goes to the charts, their stated goal is to stick to their system and only take trades inside their trading parameters however their unstated goal is that they want to make money today.

My suggestion is that your overall goal should be to be a great trader and then you are more likely to identify with how a great trader would react in certain difficult situations.

A great trader will not trade outside their system because their identity as a great trader is more important to them than making money today. It's a subtle shift but it can have a huge impact on your trading performance.

Reacting like a Robot

The advantage human traders have over robots is that they can make more connections and thus make more sophisticated trading decisions, however the disadvantage is they are subject to emotion. In order to trade well the trader needs to think like a human but react like a robot. How can a human being react like a robot, well it is much easier if their trading goal is to react as a robot would react to a series of losses, if you are in doubt of what to do, just ask yourself what would the robot do? The robot would act in line with their trading system they have been programmed with. The only time the robot would react differently is if they didn't have the correct reaction programmed in to deal with a specific situation.

157

You may not find that assuming the identity of either a Great trader or a Trading Robot a useful trading identity, in that case adopt an identity that works for you, it could be a great sportsman or any of your heroes who would act in the way that you would wish to act in a difficult situation. Then ask yourself if 'Name' was in this situation what would they do?

Use Visualization to Practice the Correct Response

By using visualization you can mentally practice the correct response to every situation that would normally cause you to over-trade. By practicing the correct response hundreds of times you will have hardwired it into your neurology. It will then become the default response when the same event occurs again while live trading. This is the same type of practice as airline pilots, who have to practice their response to extreme situations in a simulator so they can automatically respond with the correct pre-prepared strategy in a crisis.

Over-trading and Time Frame

In this book I have mainly talked about day trading in reference to over- trading and that is because it is well recognized is that when you trade the longer time frames it is much easier to maintain self –control and refrain from over-trading. The reason is that the longer time frames use checking rather than watching. What I mean by that is that there are very short periods actually spent watching the charts which exposes the trader to a lot less emotional stress. In an End of Day System the time spent watching the charts could be as little as five minutes at the end of the day. It is hard to be impulsive when you have to wait a whole day to look for the next trade. Contrast that with trading the five minute chart where you spend long periods of time watching the charts with very short breaks during the trading day. So over-trading is much more a problem of day trading and spending long periods of time in front of the charts.

There are a lot of profitable trading systems, such as stock trading that rely on day-trading rather than swing trading because it is so common for stocks to gap overnight. This means that traders may be monitoring many stocks waiting for an event and have to spend many hours in front of the computer. These traders are much more likely to succumb to over-trading. By structuring their systems using aids such as text price alerts, trend-line or pattern alerts and Forced Checking, they can watch the screen when it is absolutely necessary and relax and refresh themselves while waiting for the next trading set-up.

However these strategies work equally well for those who trade the higher time frames, for example those traders who start to over-trade after a series of losses or who start watching the charts continuously when their price level has been hit. Whatever time frame you trade, if you are over-trading then strategies that outsmart your brain need to become an integral part of your trading routine.

Conclusion

Remember you are a human being, subject to the forces of behavioral economics. Your natural tendency in a trading environment is to lose control; therefore you need to be vigilant to watch your behaviors from an outside perspective to see what circumstances cause you to slip. When you find those circumstances you need to put in place strategies that will protect you from your other less well behaved self. You need to be vigilant to make sure that you don't lose control and so are not tempted to over-trade. Equally, if you are beginning to slip and take trades you shouldn't, you put in place strategies such as frequent breaks that ensure you have enough self-control left to stop over-trading in its' tracks.

In this way you can take charge of your psychology rather than letting emotions run your trading and as a result, stop over-trading forever.

All the Best and Good Trading

LR Thomas

Resources

I hope you have found this book a useful resource in your quest to improve your trading performance. If you have enjoyed this book then please leave me a review on Amazon and as a thank you I will send you a PDF copy of this book or a book of your choice.

I love to hear from my readers so if you have any comments or questions, then you can email me at lrthomasauthor@gmail.com.

Trading Mindset Video Course
'Create Your trading Success'
Go to www.traderselfcontrol.com to find out more.

If you are interested in my High ROI Trading Systems then you can visit my blog.
www.10XROItradingsystem.com
Sign up at my blog http://10XROITradingSystem.com if you would like to learn more about my High ROI Trading Systems.

You can find my video courses here..

http://10xroitradingsystem.com/video-courses/

You can find all my e-books on my Amazon author page or this page on my website.

http://10xroitradingsystem.com/the-ebooks

http://10xroitradingsystem.com/highly-recommended/

Printed in Poland
by Amazon Fulfillment
Poland Sp. z o.o., Wrocław